TAROT
The Kingdom Within

Juno Lucina and Shannon ThornFeather

For behold, the kingdom of heaven is within you.
—Luke 17:21

4880 Lower Valley Road Atglen, Pennsylvania 19310

All text and card image concepts by Juno Lucina
All illustrations by Shannon ThornFeather

Copyright © 2011 Juno Lucina and Shannon ThornFeather

Library of Congress Control Number: 2010940266

All rights reserved. No part of this work may be reproduced or used in any form or by any means—graphic, electronic, or mechanical, including photocopying or information storage and retrieval systems—without written permission from the publisher.

The scanning, uploading and distribution of this book or any part thereof via the Internet or via any other means without the permission of the publisher is illegal and punishable by law. Please purchase only authorized editions and do not participate in or encourage the electronic piracy of copyrighted materials.

"Schiffer," "Schiffer Publishing Ltd. & Design," and the "Design of pen and ink well" are registered trademarks of Schiffer Publishing Ltd.

Type set in Formal436BT /Garamond
ISBN: 978-0-7643-3711-6

Printed in China

Schiffer Books are available at special discounts for bulk purchases for sales promotions or premiums. Special editions, including personalized covers, corporate imprints, and excerpts can be created in large quantities for special needs. For more information contact the publisher:

Published by Schiffer Publishing Ltd.
4880 Lower Valley Road
Atglen, PA 19310
Phone: (610) 593-1777; Fax: (610) 593-2002
E-mail: Info@schifferbooks.com

For the largest selection of fine reference books on this and related subjects, please visit our web site at **www.schifferbooks.com**
We are always looking for people to write books on new and related subjects. If you have an idea for a book please contact us at the above address.

This book may be purchased from the publisher.
Include $5.00 for shipping.
Please try your bookstore first.
You may write for a free catalog.

In Europe, Schiffer books are distributed by
Bushwood Books
6 Marksbury Ave.
Kew Gardens
Surrey TW9 4JF England
Phone: 44 (0) 20 8392-8585; Fax: 44 (0) 20 8392-9876
E-mail: info@bushwoodbooks.co.uk
Website: www.bushwoodbooks.co.uk

Dedication

Dedicated to the Kingdom within us All.

Acknowledgments

First and foremost, thanks to Schiffer Publishing for offering *The Kingdom Within Tarot* a publishing home, and special thanks to Dinah Roseberry, our editor, for guiding us so faithfully through the process of publication. Thanks to Ferol Humphrey, for suggesting we contact Schiffer.

A special thanks to Barbara Rapp and the Los Angeles Tarot Symposium (LATS) for giving *The Kingdom Within Tarot* its first public forum.

Our heartfelt gratitude to: Lon Milo DuQuette for embracing *The Kingdom Within Tarot's* basis upon the work of Frater Achad; Mary Greer and Rachel Pollack for believing in this deck, as well as their inspiration and encouragement; Ava Park and the Goddess Temple of Orange County for their enthusiasm; Marcelina and John De Lorez for introducing us in the first place.

Thanks to Frater Achad and Frater Perdurabo for their revolutionary Qabalistic Tarot.

Unending phileo, agape, and amour to our loved ones…your stars provided us the light we needed to complete this monumental task.

Finally, a resounding AMEN to All That Is.

Contents

INTRODUCTION

CHAPTER ONE: The Major Arcana
    0 The Fool.....*9*
    1 The Magician.....*10*
    2 The High Priestess.....*13*
    3 The Empress.....*15*
    4 The Emperor.....*17*
    5 The Hierophant.....*19*
    6 The Lovers.....*21*
    7 The Chariot.....*23*
    8 Strength.....*24*
    9 The Hermit.....*26*
    10 The Wheel of Fortune.....*28*
    11 Justice.....*30*
    12 The Hanged Man.....*32*
    13 Death.....*34*
    14 Temperance.....*36*
    15 The Devil.....*38*
    16 The Tower.....*40*
    17 The Star.....*42*
    18 The Moon.....*44*
    19 The Sun.....*46*
    20 The Judgment.....*48*
    21 The World.....*50*
    Kingdom Within All.....*52*

CHAPTER TWO: The Court Cards
   Three Basic Interpretations
      Method One: Level of Power
      Method Two: Sign Correspondence   ...*59-61*
      Method Three: Actual People
  Reversed Court Cards
  Card Analysis Classification
  Archetypes *62-65*
  Minor Arcana Connection
  Seasons and Celebrations
  The Myers-Briggs® Connection
  King of Pentacles: Father Time.....*66*
  Queen of Pentacles: Mary the Virgin Mother.....*68*
  Prince of Pentacles: The Oak King (Holly King).....*70*
  Page of Pentacles: The Newborn King.....*72*
  King of Wands: Jesus Christ.....*74*
  Queen of Wands: Eostre.....*76*
  Prince of Wands: Dionysus.....*78*
  Page of Wands: Mary Magdalene.....*80*
  King of Cups: The Green Man.....*83*
  Queen of Cups: Gaia, Mother Earth.....*86*
  Prince of Cups: Sir Galahad.....*88*
  Page of Cups: Faerie Puck.....*90*
  King of Swords: Mictlantecutli.....*92*
  Queen of Swords: Hecate.....*95*
  Prince of Swords: The Lord of Misrule.....*97*
  Page of Swords: Persephone.....*99*

CHAPTER THREE: The Minor Arcana
  The Pentacles Suit.....*105*
  The Wands Suit.....*119*
  The Cups Suit.....*134*
  The Swords Suit.....*149*

CHAPTER FOUR: Tarot Spreads
  The Triangle Spread.....*169*
  The Cross Spread.....*170*
  Questions Requiring *Yes* and *No* Answers ...*172*
  Questions of Time

Conclusion.....*174*

About the Author/Illustrator.....*176*

Introduction

WELCOME TO A VERY UNIQUE TAROT DECK—one that, quite possibly, will unveil the mysteries of the Tarot like no deck you've used or book you've read before. *The Kingdom Within Tarot* was crafted to visually depict the Tarot's archetypal roots in every image—from the ancient systems of astrology and Qabalah, to humanity's universal archetypes and sacred myths, *The Kingdom Within Tarot* tenderly helps us begin to remove our own spiritual blindfolds that hide the truth from us. Through this synthesis of the essential foundations of the Tarot we form, not only a practical method of divination to help you reclaim the truth for yourself, but also an accurate map to guide you in remembering and reawakening to the absolute, the divine, and ultimately restoring your own *Kingdom Within*. In fact, *The Kingdom Within Tarot* deck is so-named because it is a tool for you to uncover these truths.

Everything you need for reading The Kingdom Within Tarot deck is included in these pages; however, the topic of Tarot itself far surpasses the space available for a deck's companion book. For the serious seeker, a much longer and in-depth study of the Tarot with regards to astrology, Qabalah, and its mythic archetypes has been jointly published by the Schiffer Publishing Group entitled, *The Alchemy of Tarot: Practical Enlightenment through the Astrology, Qabalah, and Archetypes of Tarot*. Building upon the images from *The Kingdom Within Tarot* deck, this comprehensive book explores all aspects of the Tarot to completion.

Anyone who has studied Qabalah prior to working with *The Kingdom Within Tarot* will quickly recognize that these Paths on the Qabalistic Tree of Life do not correspond to the traditional Paths as they are generally taught by many metaphysical texts at present. The Paths of *The Kingdom Within Tarot* are distinctive in that they are based upon the *Restored Tree of Life* as put forth by Aleister Crowley's star initiate, Charles Stansfield Jones, from his two ground-breaking manuscripts: *Q.B.L.* (or *The Bride's Reception*) and *The Egyptian Revival* (or *The Ever-Coming Son in The Light of The Tarot*.) Both may be found on the Internet for the curious scholar; both are public domain.

THE SPHERES

In *The Kingdom Within Tarot,* you will see a colored sphere in the **upper left corner (UL)** of each Major Arcana card, with a different-colored sphere in the **lower right corner (LR)**. These are each card's correlation to its Path on the Qabalistic Tree of Life: the colored spheres on each card stand for the two of the ten Sephiroth that are joined by the Path of a particular trump.

In each of the four corners of the COURT CARDS you will notice a colored sphere:

THE KINGS have four grey spheres (for their correlation with Chokmah, the Father) in each corner.
THE QUEENS have four black spheres (for Binah, the Mother).
THE PRINCES have four golden spheres (for Tiphereth, the Son).
THE PAGES have four spheres divided into equal colors of russet, navy, citrine, and olive (for Malkuth, the Daughter).

At the bottom center of each of the Minor Arcana cards there is half of a colored sphere, representing one of the Sephirah on the Tree of Life. Qabalistically speaking, the number of a Minor Arcana card (or pips as they have often been called) has a correlation to one of the Sephiroth on the Tree of Life.

For more information about these colored spheres, their correlation to Qabalah, and their use within Tarot readings, please refer to my broader exploration of the Tarot entitled, *The Alchemy of Tarot: Practical Enlightenment through the Astrology, Qabalah, and Archetypes of Tarot*. Although this book shares some basic information about the cards and simple spreads as explored in this companion book for *The Kingdom Within Tarot* deck, these are only repeated to give the reader continuity—*The Alchemy of Tarot* takes this study much farther and deeper, exploring the astrological, Qabalistic, and archetypal roots shared by ALL Tarot decks.

Whatever your concerns, I hope that *The Kingdom Within Tarot* provides you with the tools you need to discover concise answers to your questions, as well as aids you in gaining awareness and confronting the truth of your life's circumstances. May this deck and companion book guide you towards confronting the truth of your searching and/or suffering, through the process of peeling back the fog and overwhelm that prevents you from achieving a perfect answer for each and all.

Chapter One

The Major Arcana

0 The Fool
– Uranus –

Path 11: Malkuth to Yesod
Aleph – א : Ox / 1 / A

Description of Illustration:
A dangerously wild child—clearly uncontrollable—with a knapsack over his shoulder, has one foot on the planet Uranus and one foot entering the abyss of outer space. A swan, pierced by the Fool's arrow and discarded bow, plummets ahead of him as he literally bristles with electricity and leaves tornadoes, lightning, and earthquakes in his wake. UL sphere is purple (Yesod) while LR sphere is divided into four equal colors of russet, navy, citrine, and olive (Malkuth).

Astrological Meaning: The Unexpected
   Element: Air, Androgynous
   Rules: Aquarius
   Minor Arcana Association: Swords Suit (Air)

Key Phrases:
- A force beyond your control—BE CAREFUL!
- Unexpected events for good or evil.
- Uranus shatters and destroys all boundaries—from disease, to divorce, to revolutions.
- Uncontrollable disasters such as tornadoes, lightning, earthquakes, or accidents.
- The pure, unadulterated wildness of children.

- Folly, eccentricity, even mania.
- Places that are far away and out of reach.
- Power and power plants; technology, electricity, and electronics; Uranium.
- The nervous system, circulation of the blood, and pineal gland. Sudden illnesses, growths, or spasms (like epilepsy or a paralyzing stroke), sudden falls; accidents due to electricity, explosions, lightning, or natural disasters.

UPRIGHT DIVINATORY MEANING:

The Fool always warns us to BE CAREFUL! It warns of something unexpected and uncontrollable entering our lives, possibly on a worldwide scale. Something will be dissolving or disintegrating—to know what, look at the surrounding cards. (For example, if The Fool ends up next to Justice or Cancer, it can show the disintegration of a relationship, marriage, or home.) The Fool can also represent a child in the querent's life, places or things beyond the querent's reach, and natural disasters. If well aspected, these catastrophic changes will ultimately be for the benefit of the querent; if poorly aspected, they will be to the querent's detriment.

REVERSED DIVINATORY MEANING:

The querent may be fearful of things out of his or her control, or else the querent IS out of control. Sometimes this may warn the reader to be cautious of the querent, especially if surrounded by dangerous cards (like the Hanged Man or the Judgment). The inner life of the querent is chaotic, wild, and volatile. The querent wants drastic change. Conversely, the querent may be concerned about a child or world events that are out of his/her control.

1 The Magician
– Mercury –

PATH 12: MALKUTH TO HOD
BETH – ב : HOUSE / 2 / B

DESCRIPTION OF ILLUSTRATION:

An impressive image of the planet Mercury with an all-knowing face is surrounded by eight doves and raised upon a dais before an awed audience who listens with rapt attention as he instructs them, vaguely reminiscent of *The Wizard of Oz*. Off to the left and partially concealed behind a curtain is the messenger god Hermes, the creator of the illusion of the god-like Mercurian image. Hermes is in disguise himself, for although he holds his caduceus and wears his characteristic winged sandals and hat, he has added these wings to the tuxedo and black top hat of a common street magician. UL sphere is orange (Hod) while LR sphere is divided into four equal colors of russet, navy, citrine, and olive (Malkuth).

ASTROLOGICAL MEANING: THE CONNECTOR

Element: Air, Androgynous
Rules: Gemini and Virgo (although some astrologers believe that the natural ruler of Virgo was the planet that was destroyed and is now the asteroid belt)
Minor Arcana Association: 8 Wands, 5 Pentacles, 10 Pentacles, 3 Cups, 6 Swords.

KEY PHRASES:

- Signifies an important message for the querent's life, for the Roman god Mercury is the great messenger of the gods.
- The intellect, learning, and the mind; therefore, Mercury's greatest strength is also his greatest weakness, for although he is clever and excels at categorizing, he tends to be harsh, cold, rationalizing, and calculating, with no emotions.
- Mercury makes moving connections: He moves information from one place to another, like oral speech, telephone conversations, mailed letters, translations, messengers, and email.
- Mercury works well with numbers, such as in math, computers, and statistics.
- Paperwork, credentials, words, and perjury (transgressions resulting from words).
- Moving modes of transportation that make connections between one place and another: cars, bikes, planes, etc. Also, traveling short distances.
- The left hemisphere (the logical, analytical portion) of the brain, along with arms, legs, shoulders, the lungs, the eyes, and the tongue.
- If adversely aspected, signifies illnesses associated with thinking and communication: brain tumor, headaches, stammering tongue, delusions, memory problems, insanity, dumbness, etc.
- Adaptable, mercurial, changeable, wishy-washy, bi-sexual, and confusing.
- Strongly influenced by the other planets and easily swayed by outside events or on a whim.
- Skill, wisdom, adaptation, subtlety, craft, cunning; some-

times occult wisdom because of the association with the Greek god, Hermes, and the Egyptian god, Thoth.
- Trickster, juggler, sexual difficulties.
- Places of communication and thinking, such as schools, telephone companies, Internet providers, newspapers, etc.
- Small animals and veterinarians.
- Alchemically, Mercury rules the metal mercury.

UPRIGHT DIVINATORY MEANING:

At its most basic level, this card warns that the querent needs to listen carefully to the message of the reading, for it contains crucial information to the querent's life. If well placed, it suggests that the querent should continue to be logical, rational, and objective in the situation—the energy of the Magician will aid the querent in seeing the truth and making the necessary connections to attain his or her goal. However, if poorly placed, this card signifies that the querent is lost in his or her illusions of justification and rationalization, using the artificial constructs of intellect to avoid seeing the truth of the matter.

At a more advanced divinatory level, the upright Magician can signify that the energy of the planet Mercury is surrounding the querent, affecting his or her life (see Key Phrases above). If poorly placed, then the difficulties or illnesses associated with the planet Mercury are manifesting. If well placed, then the positive aspects of the energy of Mercury are apparent. It can warn of a trickster in the querent's life. The Magician can also emphasize an important message or communication, as well as herald an upcoming trip.

REVERSED DIVINATORY MEANING:

The querent is seeking wisdom, and education, perhaps even a teacher; the querent needs knowledge and realizes it. A reversed card can also show that the energy of the Magician is originating within the querent…either trapped and attempting to get out, or else on its way out but not yet manifesting in the external world. The querent may be confused, wishy-washy, and waffling back and forth with regards to the subject at hand. A reversed Magician also says that the querent's actions are a result of deliberate craft and cunning on his or her part, even though they may seem unintentional to the outside observer.

2 The High Priestess
– Moon –

Path 13: Yesod to Hod
Gimel – ג : Camel, Rope / 3 / G

Description of Illustration:

A Hindu woman, reminiscent of the goddess Shakti, squats as though birthing. On her forehead is the Silver Star. Below her is her manifestation, the Qabalistic Tree of Life to which she has just given birth. Surrounding her is the cycle of the moon—on her right the new moon, above the waxing half moon, the full moon to her left, and the waning half moon below the Tree of Life. Behind her are nine stars of the Star Universe. UL sphere is Orange (Hod) while LR sphere is purple (Yesod).

Astrological Meaning: The Initiatrix
  Element: Water, Feminine
  Rules: Cancer
  Minor Arcana Association: 9 Wands, 6 Pentacles, 4 Cups, 2 Swords, 7 Swords

Key Phrases:
- The Moon signifies the birth of all things; she is the initiator, the verb.
- She is cyclical in nature and represents the feminine cycles; she rules our emotions and our subconscious.

- She is protective and nurturing, governing home, pregnancy, and children.
- She heralds change, alteration, increase or decrease, and fluctuation. (Whether it is desirable or undesirable depends upon the surrounding cards.)
- She regenerates and manifests; she reveals significance.
- Every woman is a Moon; therefore, the High Priestess may represent a woman (especially a young woman).
- She is moody like the tides and reflects the light of those around her.
- If poorly aspected (void of course), there is nothing that can be done to alter the situation; now is not the time to act.
- The Moon suggests that you will either obtain something or that you will have an upcoming move or initiation.
- Any place or job connected with water or women—rivers, ponds, baths, bogs, sailors, gynecologists, etc.
- Stomach, womb, breasts, the left eye of men and right eye of women.
- Alchemically, the Moon rules silver.

UPRIGHT DIVINATORY MEANING:

The High Priestess reveals the querent's powers of manifestation and regeneration. She is always a powerful influence in a reading and never to be taken lightly, for she reveals the "verb," the action, the direction of the querent at this present moment. At its most basic level, an upright High Priestess says that the querent is in his or her prime or at the height of his or her powers (a full moon) with regards to the subject under consideration. The Priestess reveals the emotional world of the querent, and always points towards the most significant portion of the reading—to help determine this area of significance, look at the surrounding cards. If well aspected, the High Priestess communicates that now is the time to act; if poorly aspected, she warns the querent that now is not the time. The High Priestess portends an upcoming birth—whether the literal birth of a child or the figurative birth of a goal of the querent's depends upon the surrounding cards; the High Priestess may even portend the "birth" of an upcoming move.

REVERSED DIVINATORY MEANING:

If this card is reversed, the querent has lots of potential growth before him or her (a new moon) with regards to the subject at hand. It also reveals moodiness and emotionalism on the part of the querent. The querent longs to give birth to something (whether to a goal or an actual child depends upon surrounding cards) but is struggling to manifest the creation. A reversed High Priestess tells the querent to look deeply within him—or herself—it suggests that this is a time of introspection, a time to prepare and regenerate, rather than to act.

3 The Empress
– Venus –

Path 14: Malkuth to Netzach
Daleth – ד : Door / 4 / D

Description of Illustration:
A demure, enchanting Geisha glances over her shoulder at us with a come-hither look in her eyes. She stands outside in a lush Japanese garden, surrounded by the artful blending of natural beauty with refined symmetry. On either side of her we find the tantalizing images of female fertility. Down the back of her cherry-blossomed kimono are sprinkled seven butterflies, and emblazoned upon her fan is the image of the planet Venus. UL sphere is green (Netzach) while LR sphere is divided into four equal colors of russet, navy, citrine, and olive (Malkuth).

Astrological Meaning: The Lover
Element: Earth, Feminine
Rules: Taurus, Libra (although some astrologers speculate that when we discover a tenth planet, it will actually be the natural ruler of Libra)
Minor Arcana Association: 4 Wands, 9 Pentacles, 2 Cups, 7 Cups, 5 Swords

Key Phrases:
- Venus is the Lesser Benefic; everything tends to get better when Venus appears in a reading.
- Increases happiness, success, pleasure, luxury, prosperity, artistic value, and monetary situation. Rules affection, love, amusement, and enjoyment.
- Venus is womanhood at its best; sometimes she represents pregnancy, but the emphasis is upon fertility rather than regeneration (as with the Moon.) Also wives and mothers.
- Venus is female sexuality and tantalizing temptation.
- Anything beautiful and alluring—lovely young women, flowers, jewelry, perfume, art, musical instruments, etc.
- Any work associated with beauty or aesthetics—jewelers, musicians, songs, decorators, female adornment, and beauty items (including purses and cash).
- Any location that is beautiful and alluring—gardens, outdoors, meadows, fountains, bedrooms, beds, wardrobes, cushions, dancing schools, places connected with beauty and art.
- If poorly aspected, Venus is extravagant, careless, lazy, without credit or repute, as well as inclined to inappropriate bedfellows and dissipation.
- Back, belly, veins, hernias, female reproductive organs, and the skin (as it beautifies us).
- Alchemically, Venus rules copper.

Upright Divinatory Meaning:
The Empress is a beautiful card, literally; she beautifies and sweetens the surrounding cards and situation whenever she shows up in a reading. In a man's reading, she can represent his mother or lover, as well as suggest a potential lover entering his life. In a woman's reading she suggests that the querent is a wonderful woman and mother; she may also indicate that the woman is fertile and able to become pregnant (or perhaps is already so). As a significator, she points towards locations and professions dealing with fertility, beauty, or aesthetics; perhaps the querent is an artist, or loves jewelry, or is a stay-at-home mom. Because Venus rules Taurus, she may also appear in a reading to "sweeten up" the querent's money matters. In a reading regarding love, The Empress brings feminine romance and seduction in contrast to the more masculine raw, animal passion. If very poorly aspected, The Empress suggests loss and dissipation in the areas that Venus normally "sweetens."

Reversed Divinatory Meaning:
When the Empress is reversed in a woman's reading, the querent is longing to experience the full blessings of womanhood, but feels thwarted in some way. Perhaps she is looking for love, feels she lacks beauty or attractiveness, longs to become a mother, or feels as though her current partner does not satisfy her needs as a woman. She may even feel stifled by her own mother. In a man's reading, the Empress reversed suggests a seeking for feminine energy to complete his life—longing for a lover or love affair, or else he may be concerned about his wife or mother. In this position the Empress may also reveal the querent's financial concerns and longing for greater resources—a wishing for the nurturing abundance and security of Mother Earth. If very poorly aspected, the Empress can suggest that the querent is lazy, extravagant, and inclined to wanton and lascivious behavior.

4 The Emperor
– Aries –

PATH 21: TIPHERETH TO GEBURAH
HEH – ה : WINDOW / 5 / H

DESCRIPTION OF ILLUSTRATION:
It is sunrise as a red Samurai Warrior, right out of feudal Japan, rides an enormous ram, poised to attack us. He holds the planet Mars high in his right hand to throw at his enemy, as his left hand spears the very ram upon which he rides. UL sphere is red (Geburah) while LR sphere is yellow (Tiphereth).

ASTROLOGICAL MEANING: THE RAM

    Element: Fire, Masculine, Transmissive, Cardinal sign
    Ruled by: Mars
    Minor Arcana Association: 2, 3, 4 of Wands

KEY PHRASES:
- The Sun is in Aries from March 20th to April 19th.
- First sign of the Zodiac; has a natural affinity with the First House.
- New starts or beginnings (sunrise); immediate past or future.
- Aries is powerful, aggressive, and authoritative; therefore, it is associated with war, conquest, victory, strife and ambition.
- Shows the length of life of the querent.

- Aries brings you back to yourself, so it is excellent for Pathworking.
- The father and fatherhood.
- Rules engineering, architecture, athletics, mechanics, the military, and construction.
- Rules sharp peaks or mountains, pastures, hiding places, isolated places, angry animals, any competitions or sports, and iron.
- Rules the head and face, and any related maladies (i.e., pimples, disfigurements, headaches, baldness, etc). Also the blood and muscles.

UPRIGHT DIVINATORY MEANING:

The Emperor heralds something beginning in the querent's life, as well as anything immediate in the querent's life. The Emperor suggests a powerful, aggressive authority figure, whether it is the querent himself or a person in the querent's life depends upon the Emperor's position and surrounding cards in the spread. It often signifies the querent's father; in a man's reading it may discuss the querent himself as a father, or in a woman's reading it may discuss the father of her children. In questions of health, the Emperor discusses the head and the length of the querent's life, as well as any questions of conflict, war, or competition, wherein the querent is generally victorious if the Emperor is well aspected. If poorly aspected, this card can warn of an angry, potentially violent man in the querent's life, as well as problems with any of the areas governed by Aries.

REVERSED DIVINATORY MEANING:

The reversed Emperor addresses who and what the querent really is, once all the facades and actions are stripped away; the surrounding cards may reveal what the querent needs to focus upon in order to return to himself. Perhaps the querent wishes to become a father, or has worries about his children; conversely, the querent may be worried by or about his or her father or the father of her children. The querent may desire to start something new, to take up a position of leadership, or may be concerned about how long she/he will live. When well aspected, the Emperor reversed suggests that the querent is seeking power and wishes to be an effective leader. When poorly aspected, the Emperor reversed warns that the querent is power-hungry, conflictive, and possibly inclined towards violence and rage.

5 The Hierophant
– Taurus –

PATH 16: HOD TO NETZACH
VAV – ו : NAIL / 6 / V, O, U

DESCRIPTION OF ILLUSTRATION:
In an ornate cathedral, a wealthy Elizabethan patron gives money to a struggling young artist to support his artistic creation. The artist sculpts an impressive image of a large, handsome bull. The patron wears the green orb of the planet Venus on his ring finger and carries the staff of the three ages (Isis, Osiris, and Horus) in his right hand. UL sphere is green (Netzach) while LR sphere is orange (Hod).

ASTROLOGICAL MEANING: THE BULL
  Element: Earth, Feminine, Receptive, Fixed sign
  Ruled by: Venus
  Minor Arcana Association: 5, 6, 7 of Pentacles

KEY PHRASES:
- The Sun is in Taurus from April 19th to May 20th.
- Second sign of the Zodiac; has a natural affinity with the Second House.
- Resources on all levels to accomplish the querent's goals. (Why associate the Bull with resources and money? Ancient man used cattle as the first recorded medium of exchange; the Greeks valued items for trade by heads of cattle, and the

Romans placed the image of an Ox upon their coins. Even our English words for coin and capital are based upon the Latin words for cattle and property.)
- The querent's money, finances, and investments; natural talents or gifts.
- Represents a professional or expert in his/her field; this card either indicates that the querent is a professional, or else it suggests that the querent needs to consult a professional, such as a doctor or lawyer.
- Rules lawsuits initiated by the querent, the querent's resources in a lawsuit, and the lawyer hired by the querent.
- Slow to change.
- Because of its connection with Venus, Taurus rules fashion and beauty experts, landscapers, artist, musicians, and designers. Also banking, investing, and landowners.
- Rules hidden places of the Earth, like forests, caves, and mines, also farm buildings, pasture, countryside, and cellars.
- The neck and throat and any maladies affecting the throat; a fine singing voice.

Upright Divinatory Meaning:

At the basic level, the Hierophant speaks of security and those things that serve as our foundation—physical, financial, and emotional resources. The Hierophant points towards the control societal standards exert over us. When well placed, it suggests successful financial endeavors and an increase in resources and prosperity; however, when poorly placed, there will be problems with resources or the financial difficulties will continue in the querent's life. An upright Hierophant may also tell the querent that it's time to seek an expert's advice (such as a lawyer, psychologist, doctor, or financial consultant) in the area under consideration. As the querent's significator, this indicates that the querent is at the top of his field and has a worthy professional reputation; she/he is highly successful in his or her career. When well aspected, this card can indicate winning a lawsuit. If poorly aspected, this card often reveals a querent to be stuck in the monotony of day-to-day survival, weighed down by the obligations of pleasing those in authority.

Reversed Divinatory Meaning:

In order to establish stability, the querent is turning towards external authority figures (teachers, clergy, experts, politicians) to prescribe how she/he must live rather than trusting him or herself, willingly abiding by the standards and restrictions of culture, education, religion, economics, and patriotism in order to be "right" or "good." The Hierophant reversed also often shows that the querent is worried about resources and is trying to make more money; perhaps she/he is even considering consulting a professional about a particular area of concern. The querent might be resisting a change in his or her life that seems imminent or necessary. Additionally, she/he may be worried about his or her reputation, or else seeking to become a professional and begin a career in one of the areas associated with Taurus.

6 The Lovers
– Gemini –

Path 17: Hod to Tiphereth
Zain – ז : Sword / 7 / Z

Description of Illustration:

In a scene reminiscent of Plato's Cave, a lighter boy and a darker girl (who otherwise could be twins) watch a romantic movie in a theatre. In the seats around them are couples involved in various stages of relationship—kissing, quarreling, silent separation, and adultery. But the boy and girl are oblivious as we see the image that they are each envisioning of the other projected onto the screen—he is her Knight in Shining Armor and she is his Perfect Princess. On the screen they are twin souls, and the planet Mercury shines like a great Cupid above them—holding the Bow of the Crescent Moon and the Arrow of Sagittarius—between the imaginary film lovers, winking conspiratorially. UL sphere is yellow (Tiphereth) while LR sphere is orange (Hod).

Astrological Meaning: The Twins

   Element: Air, Masculine, Transmissive, Mutable sign
   Ruled by: Mercury
   Minor Arcana Association: 8, 9, 10 of Swords

Key Phrases:
- The Sun is in Gemini from May 20th to June 20th.
- Third sign of the Zodiac; has a natural affinity with the Third House.
- Gemini represents our reflection in the mirror—not what we really are, but what we seem to be; therefore it rules the querent's image, the surface, and the superficial. Also the skin.
- Rules infatuation and puppy love—the love of the reflection of oneself in the other.
- Because of its connection with twins, it rules twins and many parts of the body that come in pairs—arms, eyes, hands, lungs, shoulders. Also brothers and sisters.
- Because of its emphasis upon image, Gemini rules image-conscious professions like acting, fashion, stage, television, and movies.
- Because of its bond with Mercury it rules students, writers, public speakers, teachers, and secondary schools, as well as data, information, computers, and the Internet.
- Any written or verbal contract or communication.
- Rules veins, arteries, and nerves…since they connect all the systems of the body.
- Rules high, airy places, like hilltops, mountaintops, upstairs rooms, and skyscrapers.
- Rules places of connection like hallways and windows; places of communication like rooms for debating, reading, or writing. Also storage places, like chests, boxes, or computer memory.
- Smaller living spaces, like apartments and condominiums; traveling or moving a short distance.
- Never long term, maximum 12-18 months.

Upright Divinatory Meaning:
At the initial level, the Lovers discusses the appearance of the matter, the querent's image, or the world's surface perception of him or her. It can refer to a communication that has occurred or needs to occur. In a question of romance, the Lovers indicates a passionate, all-consuming infatuation that will not last long—for each is in love with the image of the beloved and the beauty felt in their union, rather than an awareness of the true self of the other. The Lovers generally indicates a short duration of the matter at hand, no longer than 12 to 18 months. The Lovers can signify any area governed by Gemini. If poorly aspected, this card can suggest a problem with paperwork, communication, contracts, or proper credentials.

Reversed Divinatory Meaning:
The Lovers reversed indicates that the querent is concerned about a message, his brother or sister, a contract, his or her image or looks, a lover, or something else that Gemini rules. This may also suggest that the querent is lost in infatuation. It can also indicate that, quite honestly, the querent lacks depth or perceptive insight in some crucial way. A poorly aspected Lovers can even suggest that the querent is concerned about his or her acne or wrinkles (the skin—the surface).

7 The Chariot
– Cancer –

Path 15: Yesod to Netzach
Cheth – ח : Fence / 8 / C, Ch

Description of Illustration:
It is dusk, and a Mother proudly drives her mini-van that is full of nine busy children as she pulls into the driveway in front of her home, where her husband stands with the door open to welcome his family. Two majestic sphinx statues, one white and the other black, recline on either side of the house's entrance; a gravestone graces the front lawn. One child has her hand out the window, clutching a large stuffed animal in the shape of a crab. The full moon, unusually large and predominant, rises above this homey scene, unique in that instead of the standard man or the rabbit in the moon, we see a craggy crab etched upon its surface. UL sphere is green (Netzach) while LR sphere is purple (Yesod).

Astrological Meaning: The Crab
   Element: Water, Feminine, Receptive, Cardinal sign
   Ruled by: Moon
   Minor Arcana Association: 2, 3, 4 of Cups

Key Phrases:
- The Sun is in Cancer from June 20th to July 22nd.
- Fourth sign of the Zodiac; has a natural affinity with the Fourth House.
- The end of the matter—this will happen. The end of a cycle.

- A matter of control and/or containment: Either someone secretly wants control, the querent needs to get control or get things contained, or else it's under control, depending upon dignity. Anything conservative or controlling.
- Represents querent's foundation—home, mother, family, children, genetics, or ancestry. Also moving one's home or traveling close to home; often a car because many people live in their car as much as they live in their home. Things close to home, like neighbors or yard.
- Any profession having to do with food, comfort, or home—like restaurants, cooking, hotel work, real estate, or homemaking.
- Watery places—lakes, harbors, moving water, beaches, seaside, springs, wells, marshes.
- Problems with water, from edema to flooding.
- Rules the stomach, mouth, womb, breasts, and women.

Upright Divinatory Meaning:

When the Chariot is upright in a reading, it reveals the foundation of the matter under consideration—what's really beneath it as well as its natural and unavoidable conclusion. This card also reveals the way to get control of a situation. The Chariot speaks of the querent's roots, home, children, and foundation; it may also refer to the querent's more nurturing parent. The Chariot may also discuss a place, problem, or occupation that is ruled by Cancer.

Reversed Divinatory Meaning:

The querent is concerned about home, mother, children, or family; she/he may also be struggling with the way things are or the ending of a cycle. Perhaps the querent feels out of control and wishes to regain control, or else she/he may be struggling with moodiness, the need to be babied, and over-sensitivity.

8 Strength
– Leo –

Path 19: Netzach to Tiphereth
Teth – ט : Serpent / 9 / T

Description of Illustration:

In an enchanted wood, a virile, solar young man rides a lion as they chase a nubile, playful young ingénue straddling a lioness; they are both naked. Behind them lies the carcass of a dead ram upon which they have just finished feasting. The Sun shines bright above them, smiling down at them as though blessing their lustful sport. UL sphere is yellow (Tiphereth) while LR sphere is green (Netzach).

Astrological Meaning: The Lion

Element: Fire, Masculine, Transmissive, Fixed sign
Ruled by: Sun
Minor Arcana Association: 5, 6, 7 of Wands

Key Phrases:
- The Sun is in Leo from July 22nd to August 22nd.
- Fifth sign of the Zodiac; has a natural affinity with the Fifth House.
- Leo is the Lord of Life; therefore, he rules our general health and physical vitality as well as the things that make life worth living for most of us—happiness, fun, and amusement.
- The querent's self esteem and luck.

- The heart, back, ribs, spine, sides, and any related illnesses, also fevers.
- Sex, lust, and desire at its most basic level, love affairs.
- Leo is primal, animalistic; it's Nature's Law.
- Any place or work that deals in fun, entertainment, or amusement—any kind of performer, the stage, bars, theatres, etc.; in the 11th house, Leo shows fame and a large public following.
- Any places that are wild, rocky, barren, or generally accessible to animals but inaccessible to humans.
- Eminent structures, like castles, national monuments, and palaces.

UPRIGHT DIVINATORY MEANING:

An upright Strength card discusses the querent's general health, vitality, and love of life. It often reveals that the querent is involved in a love affair or else portends the opportunity for one. Strength discusses a place, problem, or occupation that is ruled by Leo. If poorly aspected, Strength reveals the querent's poor health, low self-esteem, and general lack of passion and life force.

REVERSED DIVINATORY MEANING:

Strength reversed reveals the querent's desire for a potential love affair, worries about health, energy and exhaustion, or else his or her longing for fun, passion, and happiness. Perhaps the querent wants to be an entertainer. This card may also reveal what the querent lusts after. The querent may be struggling with the harsher realities of existence, and feels that she/he simply does not have the strength to withstand.

9 The Hermit
– Virgo –

Path 20: Hod to Geburah
Yod – י : Hand / 10 / Y, I, J

Description of Illustration:
 A solitary accountant, meticulously laboring at his numbers and books with a wrinkled brow, sits at his small desk in a cramped and darkened room; he is completely unaware of the bright window behind him through which Paradise awaits. On his desk are two paperweights on top of stacks and stacks of more work: The first is the planet Mercury and the second is a statue of a beautiful Virgin holding a stalk of grain. (Please note that the word virgin means "intact." A "virgin" in ancient times was a priestess to the goddess of the harvest, Demeter, in the Mediterranean temples during the golden age of Rome. She was complete in and of herself and beholden to no man for her livelihood.) The Hermit, however, shows us what happens when the Virgin gains too much dominance in our lives. UL sphere is red (Geburah) while LR sphere is orange (Hod).

Astrological Meaning: The Virgin
 Element: Earth, Feminine, Receptive, Mutable sign
 Ruled by: Mercury (although some astrologers believe that the natural ruler of Virgo was the planet that was destroyed and is now the asteroid belt)
 Minor Arcana Association: 8, 9, 10 of Pentacles

Key Phrases:
- The Sun is in Virgo from August 22nd to September 22nd.
- Sixth sign of the Zodiac; has a natural affinity with the Sixth House.
- Rules acute illnesses, as well as doctors, nurses, hospitals, and clinics.
- Rules institutions and bureaucracies.
- Rules the power of assimilation, and therefore the intestines and the lower stomach.
- Rules employees and service organizations.
- Service occupations, like secretaries, accountants, lawyers, health practitioners; any work that requires considerable attention to detail.
- Rules hidden fetishes, fixations, and compulsions, from masturbation to compulsive organizers.
- Rules both virgins and kinky sex (like bondage and S&M, wherein there is an element of punishment, atonement, or self-flagellation).
- Any place wherein work is carried out, such as offices and studies; anywhere books or merchandise are kept, such as cupboards and storerooms; any place at floor level or low down.

Upright Divinatory Meaning:
The Hermit warns us to pay attention to the particulars. Analyze the situation. Work out the details. The Hermit may also discuss illness. As the querent's significator, this card may say that the querent has a solitary nature or else suggest that the querent is in the medical profession; if poorly aspected it may suggest that the querent is lonely, of a critical nature, or sick. The Hermit may signify someone the querent has consulted (or will consult) for advice, or else discuss the value of the advice that the querent received, whether for good or ill depends upon surrounding cards. If well aspected, the Hermit suggests that the querent is denying the physical pleasures of life and ascetically "going within" to progress spiritually.

Reversed Divinatory Meaning:
The querent is stuck in a fixation. When the Hermit is reversed it often reveals the querent's worries about illness or the details of a situation; perhaps the querent feels alone and isolated when she/he doesn't want to be. There is also a longing to be perfect or complete emanating from the querent that may manifest in higher mental pursuits. The querent may also be concerned about how he makes his money.

10 The Wheel of Fortune
– Jupiter –

Path 31: Chokmah to Kether
Kaph – כ : Palm of hand / 20 / K

Description of Illustration:
 The enormous planet Jupiter fills this card; super-imposed upon it is the medieval Wheel of Fortune. At the four corners of the Wheel we find the symbols for the four fixed signs of the Zodiac: the man (Aquarius), the bull (Taurus), the lion (Leo), and the eagle (Scorpio). Around the top half of the rim of the wheel are all the blessings, joys, and sensual pleasures of life, such as food and drink, riches and gambling, lovemaking and winning, and all forms of material merriment. Around the bottom half of the rim are the flip side of the results of immersing oneself in the physical universe—loss, hangovers, obesity, sickness, conflict, stress, and depression. At the hub, however, we find an image of an eternally fat, jolly Buddha. For no matter how much the Wheel turns, no matter how many ups and downs are experienced by those on the outer rim of the wheel, those few who find their still center of wisdom—stopping the endless cycle of avoiding and seeking—will discover true bliss. UL sphere is white (Kether) while LR sphere is gray (Chokmah).

Astrological Meaning: The Expander
 Element: Air, Masculine

Rules: Sagittarius, Pisces (classical astrologers consider Jupiter to share rulership of Pisces with Neptune)

Minor Arcana Association: 6 Wands, 2 Pentacles, 9 Cups, 4 Swords, 8 Swords

Key Phrases:

- Jupiter is the Greater Benefic; it enlarges all that it touches (from your money to your waistline).
- Brings good fortune, luck, prosperity, grandeur, and growth.
- Rules divine power, blessings, spirituality; your destiny as opposed to your future.
- Rules the liver, hips, thighs, sciatic nerve, the pituitary gland, and any illness resulting from too much good living.
- If poorly aspected, Jupiter can bring intoxication and excess—whether from celebration, riches, comfort, success, or eminence.
- Rules jobs requiring just judgment—judges, senators, councilors, clergy, lawyers; also foreigners and middle-aged men.
- Rules sweet scents and large gentle animals, such as horses and whales.
- Rules grand, large places, such as courts, important public places, and foreign places.
- Also rules spiritual places, like altars, churches, and cathedrals.
- Rules gambling, horse race jockeys, and the winner in any matter.
- Alchemically, Jupiter rules tin.

Upright Divinatory Meaning:

The Wheel of Fortune returns us to our divine source, to our destiny, to truth. It always speaks of expansion, growth, progression, blessings, and spirituality; perhaps the querent is entering a phase of growth, learning, and focusing on spiritual pursuits; the querent's concerns will be alleviated and a period of prosperity is at hand. When well aspected, the Wheel signifies vast expansion of blessings in the querent's life; when poorly aspected, however, it warns of excess and its painful consequences. The querent may have problems with the excesses of prosperity—obesity, intoxication, pride, material obsession. The Wheel, as the card of Jupiter, can also discuss divine judgment in the querent's life, whether in the courtroom, by the clergy, or through life's circumstances depends upon surrounding cards. If well aspected, it signifies the winner in the subject under discussion.

Reversed Divinatory Meaning:

The querent is filled with a longing for prosperity, blessings, and spiritual growth; perhaps she/he is concerned about an upcoming judgment, either in court or by a religious organization. The Wheel reversed can also reveal the querent's obsession with his or her weight or addictions.

11 Justice
– Libra –

Path 22: Netzach to Chesed
Lamed – ל : Ox Goad or Whip / 30 / L

Description of Illustration:
    The head of the Egyptian Goddess of balance, Ma'at, rises from the planet Venus, resting at the apex of huge, ornate scales that are balanced against the backdrop of a vibrant autumn sunset over the beach at high tide. The scales are not static, but instead are constantly moving to remain in perfect balance. On the left scale is the Sun, superimposed with the image of the lighter (male) twin from The Lovers card, while the Moon is on the right scale, superimposed with the image of the darker (female) twin; the Sun and Moon (the two twins) reach for each other. Below them is an ancient piece of parchment which reads "I, Light, and I, Darkness, do promise to…." UL sphere is blue (Chesed) while LR sphere is green (Netzach).

Astrological Meaning: The Scales
    Element: Air, Masculine, Transmissive, Cardinal sign
    Ruled by: Venus (although some astrologers speculate that when we discover a tenth planet, it will actually be the natural ruler of Libra)
    Minor Arcana Association: 2, 3, 4 of Swords

Key Phrases:
- The Sun is in Libra from September 22nd to October 22nd.
- Seventh sign of the Zodiac; has a natural affinity with the Seventh House.
- Rules marriage, equal partnerships (both business and personal), and significant others.
- Rules lawsuits, legal proceedings, and open enemies.
- Rules contracts being made or broken.
- The balance of opposing forces, as in war and places of war.
- Airplanes, airports, and anything with two wings.
- Rules the area of the body encompassing the lower back and buttocks; also the kidneys.
- Libra is called the Portal of Death, for its natural placement in the zodiac is at sunset.
- Rules high places, windy places, hillsides, mountains, upstairs, and attics, as well as one room within or joined to another.

Upright Divinatory Meaning:
The Justice card reveals the truth about the querent's partnerships; to know whether it refers to a business or personal partner, look at the surrounding cards. Saturn, Mars, Pluto, Neptune, and Uranus always afflict Libra: If any of these planets surround the Justice card, there will be serious troubles with partnerships and open enemies. When poorly aspected, Justice can discuss the dissolution of a partnership; conversely, when well aspected it can show a blessing in an existing partnership or even a new partnership on the horizon. Justice upright can also discuss contracts or lawsuits in which the querent is involved. Occasionally, this card can indicate ending, completion, or death, but only with the appropriate surrounding cards.

Reversed Divinatory Meaning:
There is a need for balance in the querent's life. Justice reversed reveals the querent's worries or longings about partnerships; perhaps she/he is worried about a partner or else desires to begin a new partnership. The reversed Justice also discusses the querent's concerns with regards to any of the topics ruled by Libra.

12 The Hanged Man
– Neptune –

Path 18: Yesod to Tiphereth
Mem – מ : Seas or Water / 40 / M

DESCRIPTION OF ILLUSTRATION:
A swashbuckling pirate holds a blindfolded man's ankle as he dangles the doomed man upside down over the side of his pirate ship; one of the legs of the upside down man is bent perpendicular, causing his legs to form a cross. His arms are outstretched, each hand in a purple halo, making a reversed triangle with his head as the apex, encircled by a golden halo. Thus, the cross surmounts the triangle. Sharks eagerly wait in the waters below the blindfolded man's head; the man foolishly smiles as though unaware of his impending fate. Oddly enough, The Hanged Man's reflection in the water beneath him is brighter than the murky depths. In place of the traditional skull and cross bones, the billowing sail boasts the image of the planet Neptune with crossed bones behind it. Everything is covered by wisps of fog that make it difficult to see various parts of the scene. UL sphere is yellow (Tiphereth) while LR sphere is purple (Yesod).

ASTROLOGICAL MEANING: THE VISIONARY
  Element: Water, Androgynous
  Rules: Pisces (astrologers consider Neptune to share rulership with Jupiter)
  Minor Arcana Association: Cups Suit (Water)

Key Phrases:
- Positively speaking, Neptune rules imagination, poetry, otherworldly artists, psychics, fantasy, science fiction, visions, and visionaries.
- Negatively speaking, Neptune is known for its lack of earthly reality, illusion, inconstancy, impracticality, delusion, swindling, and deception.
- Neptune signifies fog, drugs, gasses, and drug addicts.
- Neptune, like Uranus, moves us towards the future; however, it operates through the water element, thus using emotion, intuition, and psychic force to shake things up. Where Uranus dissipates (like air) all boundaries in order to make a new world, Neptune dissolves (like water) all distinctions that prevent us from being whole.
- When Neptune is very well placed, the person is probably psychic, tending to lose him or herself in another person or in an ideal; they are also willing to sacrifice anything, including themselves, to bring their visions into reality.
- When Neptune is poorly placed, people cannot be trusted. They behave like pirates: They ignore social mores, make their own rules, and live for their own profit. Neptune tends to make us devious, unfaithful, spacey, and uncivilized.
- Rules insanity, hypnosis, sleepwalking, and fraud.
- Rules feet, weakening and debilitating illnesses, illnesses that are difficult to diagnose and treat, the thalamus, and the lymphatic system. The right hemisphere of the brain (the seat of creativity and imagination).
- Rules occupations of the sea, such as sailing, fishing, and piracy.
- Neptune turns our world upside down. Just as the Hanged Man looks at the world from an upside down position, Neptune encourages us to be imaginative and consider new vantage points (perhaps even those that we deem to be "fiction").

Upright Divinatory Meaning:

If well aspected, this card signifies the power of redeeming love over self-sacrifice: choosing to enter the darkness of the unknown in order to find the light of awareness. When the Hanged Man is upright, the querent is generally lost in a fog, caught in delusion. The Hanged Man warns that the querent's head is in the clouds; they are either hiding or missing something. It can also suggest that someone is going to trick or "pull the wool" over the querent's eyes. If poorly aspected, it may warn the reader that the querent is not to be trusted, as she/he is manifesting the negative energy of Neptune. Conversely, a positive placement could suggest that the querent is a poet or a science fiction writer.

Reversed Divinatory Meaning:

The querent is deluding either himself or another, or else is worried about the unknown, deception, or lost ideals. If poorly aspected, the querent is untrustworthy and manifests all the negative attributes of Neptune. If well aspected, the querent is idealistic, dreamy, psychic, and imaginative; the reversed Hanged Man can show that the querent is actively seeking an artistic or imaginative goal. Perhaps the querent is sacrificing himself or herself for another person, or for an ideal.

13 Death
– Scorpio –

Path 24: Geburah to Chesed
Nun – נ : Fish; eagle, snake, scorpion; to sprout, to grow / 50 / N

Description of Illustration:
The Grim Reaper cuts a long silver cord with his scythe, separating the body of a dead woman who lies on the ground from her spirit that rises above her. Next to the woman's dead body are all the bills, money, and material possessions that she can't take with her, as well as the scorpion that stung and killed her. The woman's spirit grasps a snake that is shedding its skin as she focuses upon a brilliant star-like light above her. An eagle accompanies her spirit as she journeys towards the light. Within the light the planets Mars and Pluto beckon for her to join them. UL sphere is blue (Chesed) while LR sphere is red (Geburah).

Astrological Meaning: The Scorpion
Element: Water, Feminine, Receptive, Fixed sign
Ruled by: Pluto (classical astrologers consider Mars to share rulership with Pluto)
Minor Arcana Association: 5, 6, 7 of Cups

Key Phrases:
- The Sun is in Scorpio from October 22nd to November 21st.

- Eighth sign of the Zodiac; has a natural affinity with the Eighth House.
- Scorpio rules transformation, change, and growth. It moreover rules death and destruction, as they are the ultimate catalysts for transformation, change, and growth. Likewise transitions, endings, and beginnings.
- Signifies the resources of the other, whether your spouse, your business partner, or your opponent in a lawsuit; also other people's money (bills, taxes, bankruptcies, or inheritances).
- Rules anything extreme, dark, dangerous, violent, or poisonous. Places with lots of insects or reptiles as well as poisonous and stinking places. Also deep, watery, dark locations like lakes, bogs, moors, and muddy places. Rules kitchens, bathrooms, and any room that contains water; also damp places.
- Professions concerned with birthing and dying, deep and penetrating professions like psychologists and detectives, along with surgery and sanitation.
- Rules our survival issues, our reproductive urge, our desire for power and control, and our will to both destroy and create.
- Rules the groin area and organs of elimination (organs of creation and destruction) as well as the illnesses thereof.

Upright Divinatory Meaning:

Change of a life-altering nature is imminent in the querent's life; something is ending, so that something else may begin. If poorly aspected, the Death card warns of problems with bills, taxes, and debt…perhaps even a bankruptcy. If well aspected, it can speak of an inheritance or successfully overcoming credit problems. Death upright may even warn of poisoning, whether literal or figurative depends upon surrounding cards. Only very rarely does the Death card predict an ending as final as physical death, so interpret the surrounding cards very carefully before choosing this conclusion.

Reversed Divinatory Meaning:

The querent wants to change or destroy something; she/he longs for transformation. Perhaps the querent is struggling with deep safety and survival issues, or else seeks power and control. Or, maybe he's just horny. If poorly aspected, he may be worried about the money he owes or about his spouse's finances. If very poorly aspected, the querent may be worried about death or be suicidal.

14 Temperance
– Sagittarius –

Path 25: Chesed to Chokmah
Samekh – ס : Prop/ Tent peg / Tent pole / 60 / S

Description of Illustration:

A strong, wise centaur runs on the top of a high mesa in the middle of a scorching hot desert, poised with his bow and arrow ready to shoot in the direction of a graceful white swan and the planet Jupiter, far in the distance. He has clearly been traveling on a long journey, and still has far to go to make it to his destination, which appears to be the planet Jupiter. Behind him he leaves a blue female centaur who holds two cups; it seems that a fiery light shoots upwards from one cup to fill the emptiness of the other. (She's preserving the light.) UL sphere is gray (Chokmah) while LR sphere is blue (Chesed).

Astrological Meaning: The Archer
Element: Fire, Masculine, Transmissive, Mutable sign
Ruled by: Jupiter
Minor Arcana Association: 8, 9, 10 of Wands

Key Phrases:
- The Sun is in Sagittarius from November 21st to December 21st.
- Ninth sign of the Zodiac; has a natural affinity with the Ninth House

- Sagittarius rules aims, long-term goals, destinies, spirituality, and quests; it conquers.
- Rules anything far, such as exotic or foreign lands, long journeys, immigration, or diplomacy; it can also suggest something that's gone too far.
- Signifies anything high, such as philosophies, universities, or mountains.
- Governs anything hot, fast, and intense, like races, fast cars, swift horses, and jets.
- Rules the hips and thighs; also falls from horses and sports injuries.
- Rules locations that are open and high, where one can see in the distance, like the open sea; also wherever large animals live, like hills and fields. Upstairs and near fireplaces.

Upright Divinatory Meaning:

Many people wonder why the card associated with Sagittarius, a sign that is so far out and extreme, would be called "Temperance." To begin with, Temperance upright often tells querents that they are going too far and need to chill out or "temper" their current actions, or else they will crash and burn. It also speaks of the querent's goals and ambitions; to discover precisely what it is that they are aiming towards, look at the surrounding cards. The querent may be about to embark upon a long trip, or else she/he might be a foreigner. Temperance may suggest that the querent will be pursuing further education, higher philosophies, or deeper spirituality. It can even warn that the querent will get a speeding ticket.

Reversed Divinatory Meaning:

Temperance reversed reveals the querent's longing to accomplish a goal. Perhaps he wants to go on a long journey to a foreign land, return to college, or run a marathon. If poorly aspected, there might be immigration problems or the querent may simply be experiencing a state of "burn out."

15 The Devil
– Capricorn –

Path 28: Tiphereth to Binah
Ayin – ע : Eye / 70 / O

Description of Illustration:
Above a dark threshold is a stunningly beautiful angel with horns like a goat whose chest is emblazoned with an upside down pentagram. The Fallen Angel of Light hovers above the twins from the Lovers card, who are now shackled to each other as well as to all the errors from their lives that they have desperately tried to justify rather than to face. With one hand Lucifer lovingly pets a beautiful shaggy mountain goat, while the other hand points meaningfully at the couple as though to say, "As you sow, so shall you reap." The planet Saturn floats above Lucifer's head like a crown. UL sphere is black (Binah) while LR sphere is yellow (Tiphereth).

Astrological Meaning: The Goat
  Element: Earth, Feminine, Receptive, Cardinal sign
  Ruled by: Saturn
  Minor Arcana Association: 2, 3, 4 of Pentacles

Key Phrases:
- The Sun is in Capricorn from December 21st to January 20th.
- Tenth sign of the Zodiac; has a natural affinity with the Tenth House.

- Under the influence of Capricorn, each person shall reap what they've sown and pay the dues for what they've done (whether the consequences are positive or negative depends upon the individual's original deeds.)
- Capricorn rules authority figures as well as career or professional calling (as opposed to Virgo's service and servants).
- Rules one's professional reputation or standing in the world.
- Capricorn judges and controls things; therefore it rules judges, the parent who is the authority figure in the home, CEOs, bosses, administrations, government agencies, and police.
- Capricorn, sometimes called the Great Earth Mother, is the darkest, earthiest, and most material of all the signs; its influences weigh us down, cementing us to the material plane. Thus, it rules earthy, dark locations, such as mines and other places that are deep underground. Also rules mining.
- Rules bones, teeth, and knees.
- Rules farming; therefore rules anywhere animals are kept (especially goats), farm implements or places where wood is stored, barren fields, dung heaps, bushy or thorny land, and mountain paths; also places near a floor or threshold.

Upright Divinatory Meaning:

Physicality exalted to the detriment of spirituality. Just consequences (even if undesired) of a particular action or decision of the querent's. The Devil commands the querent to get control of the situation, for a great material force or temptation is propelling the querent out of control and into chaos. It may also discuss the querent's career or reputation. Upright, it often represents a boss or authority in the querent's life; with regards to a court case, it represents the judge and the judge's decision. If well aspected, it says that the querent is focused, climbing to the top of the situation at hand with hard work, or that his or her life is settled and under control. If poorly aspected, the Devil may suggest trouble with career or reputation, painful consequences as a result of poor choices, or even knee problems.

Reversed Divinatory Meaning:

Materiality and HAVING matter much more to the querent than truth or BEING. When reversed, the Devil says that the querent is worried about his or her career or standing in the world. Perhaps she/he is actively working to progress up the corporate ladder, or else is concerned about problems with an authority figure. It may also suggest that the querent is unhappy about paying the consequences for past actions.

16 The Tower
– Mars –

PATH 27: GEBURAH TO BINAH
PEH – פ : MOUTH / 80 / P

DESCRIPTION OF ILLUSTRATION:
    A tall, ominous tower looms like a perfect phallus against a dark landscape. The bright light of inner enlightenment explodes as the huge, flaming planet Mars strikes the tower, cutting it in half and releasing five magnificent lightning bolts of transformation. Five kings are thrown from the igniting Tower, two fall downwards and two sail outwards, while one flies upwards. Where Mars strikes the Tower it is covered with scorch marks and ashes, and it bleeds deep red blood. Out of Mars' destruction of the man-made apparency of the Tower rises the fiery falcon-headed Phoenix, a bird lovely and new in its natural perfection. UL sphere is black (Binah) while LR sphere is red (Geburah).

ASTROLOGICAL MEANING: THE DESTROYER
    Element: Fire, Masculine
    Rules: Aries, Scorpio (classical astrologers consider Mars to share rulership of Scorpio with Pluto)
    Minor Arcana Association: 2 Wands, 7 Wands, 5 Cups, 10 Cups, 9 Swords

Key Phrases:
- Mars is the Lesser Malefic; it attacks anything with the appearance of perfection. Mars cuts, kills, and ends all persistence.
- Mars rules accidents (often involving bloodshed), sharp objects, and violent threats.
- Rules the muscles and muscle control, blood and arteries, the male sex organs, infectious diseases and epidemics, wounds and cuts, bruises and burns; also the adrenal gland (activated when one's survival is threatened). Signifies high fevers, migraines, shingles, and frenzies.
- Mars rules activity, construction, competition, and conflict. It is the planet of anger, burning passion and ambition, war, strife, and struggle. Mars is the initiator of action; it starts things. Therefore, it starts quarrels, conflict, rage, struggles, and destruction.
- Rules anything or anyone who cuts, like surgeons; anything or anyone involved in fighting or war, like soldiers, boxers, and guns; anything or anyone who works with fire, like firemen. Mars also rules locations associated with these attributes, such as places of war, bloodshed, and destruction, as well as hot, arid places like deserts.
- When poorly aspected, Mars signifies destruction, danger, fall, and ruin.
- Often signifies an older woman in the post-menopausal or "crone" stage of life, wherein the softer, feminine energies (estrogen) of her youth have lessened as her more forceful, masculine energies (testosterone) now rise to dominance.
- Alchemically, Mars rules iron or anything with high levels of iron (like nettles and spinach); any hot or spicy food, like chili peppers and radishes; anything that grows in hot and dry places, like cactus and desert plants.

Upright Divinatory Meaning:
The Tower upright brings some sort of purifying destruction into the querent's life. Look to the surrounding cards to determine which area of the querent's life that Mars is focusing his attack. For example, coupled with Justice it might portend relational separation or divorce. If the Tower is in the sixth house or next to the Hermit, it can suggest an acute illness that is ruled by Mars, an accident, or a surgery. Surrounded by the Devil and the Hermit (or both), the Tower can warn of a soldier going to war. If well placed, it might reveal that the querent is a surgeon, or else has the ability to succeed when she/he takes action. Poorly placed, the Tower warns of ruin and possible danger in the matter under consideration. The Tower upright may also speak of an older woman in the querent's life.

Reversed Divinatory Meaning:
Look to the cards that surround the Tower reversed to discover where the querent invests his or her energy and action, what impassions and angers the querent, as well as the direction of the querent's lust and drive and zeal: it reveals that for which the querent burns. It may also discuss the querent's concern with an issue of survival. Perhaps the querent wants to enter the military or become a professional boxer or a surgeon. If poorly placed, the Tower reversed reveals the querent to be angry, uncontrollable, and dangerous. This card may also reveal the querent's worry about destruction, in general or else a specific ending.

17 The Star
– Aquarius –

Path 29: Binah to Chokmah
Tzaddi – צ : Fish hook / 90 / Tz, X

Description of Illustration:
A fantastical mermaid holds two water pitchers, one black and one grey; there are rolling hills in the distance. The black pitcher is decorated with the planet Saturn; she pours this pitcher into the ocean waves that she inhabits. The grey pitcher is emblazoned with the planet Uranus, and seems to pour straight upwards, becoming the twinkling stars in the heavens above her. The streams pouring from both pitchers look like two trees, the downward growing represents the Tree of the Knowledge of Good and Evil while the upward growing represents the Tree of Life. As we look closer, we see that the foam on the crests of the waves are in fact the huge masses of humanity, and the stream that she pours into the ocean has two tiny friends entering the world of duality together. We also see that each of the stars formed by her upward moving stream is in fact a tiny human, exuberantly free. Directly above her shines the largest star, the Dog Star, also called Sirius. UL sphere is gray (Chokmah) while LR sphere is black (Binah).

Astrological Meaning: The Water Bearer
  Element: Air, Masculine, Transmissive, Fixed sign
  Ruled by: Uranus (classical astrologers consider Saturn to share rulership with Uranus)
  Minor Arcana Association: 5, 6, 7 of Swords

Key Phrases:
- The Sun is in Aquarius from January 20th to February 18th.
- Eleventh sign of the Zodiac; has a natural affinity with the Eleventh House.
- Aquarius rules the future; it encompasses our dreams, hopes, ideals, and wishes.
- Rules anything that frees us from our bounds and restriction (i.e., democracies, revolutions, philosophies, unity, friendship, communistic brotherhood, etc.)
- Friendship, as well as the dream of love and the perfect mate.
- Open, large, pleasant places; any place that is hilly, uneven, off the floor, or near a window.
- Things have a tendency to fall in Aquarius (from the lofty heights of dreams and ideals).
- Rules large people groups, such as the public, juries, and congress. Also public service, populations, the Internet, and film.
- Rules legs, ankles, and defects of blood circulation.

Upright Divinatory Meaning:
In a reading, the Star tells us of our future, our dreams, and that which can free us from our current situation. Look to the surrounding cards to determine exactly WHAT we need to know about these topics. Aquarius generally portends a favorable future for the querent and may point to unexpected help from a friend or large people group. However, if poorly aspected, the Star can sometimes point towards dreaminess and deceived hope. Because things fall in Aquarius, the Star may also warn about an impending fall (literal or figurative) in the querent's life, and as the significator in a reading this card speaks of the querent's current fall.

Reversed Divinatory Meaning:
The querent is actively seeking a dream or ideal, something to free him or her. A reversed card can also show that the querent's dreams are trapped and unable to manifest in the external world. Poorly aspected, this card can suggest self-deception as a person values his or her ideals to the detriment of others and the facts.

18 The Moon
– Pisces –

PATH 23: TIPHERETH TO CHESED
QOPH – ק : BACK OF THE HEAD / 100 / Q

DESCRIPTION OF ILLUSTRATION:

We are looking straight down into a gazing pool in a Japanese garden. Two Koi fish, bound together like two crescent moons as they swim counter-clockwise, form a never-ending circle on the pool's surface; one fish has two planet Neptunes for eyes, and the other's eyes are two planet Jupiters. As we gaze into the nadir of the pool, we find that it is impossible to see its bottom. In the murky depths of the pool we glimpse distorted images of a sleeping man in the middle of a nightmare, an old woman gazing into a moon-like crystal ball, a man who is tied up and gagged, and a woman being burned at the stake. Hatching from a ball of dung in the center of the pool is a dazzling scarab beetle. UL sphere is blue (Chesed) while LR sphere is yellow (Tiphereth).

ASTROLOGICAL MEANING: THE FISH

Element: Water, Feminine, Receptive, Mutable sign
Ruled by: Neptune (classical astrologers consider Jupiter to share rulership with Neptune)
Minor Arcana Association: 8, 9, 10 of Cups

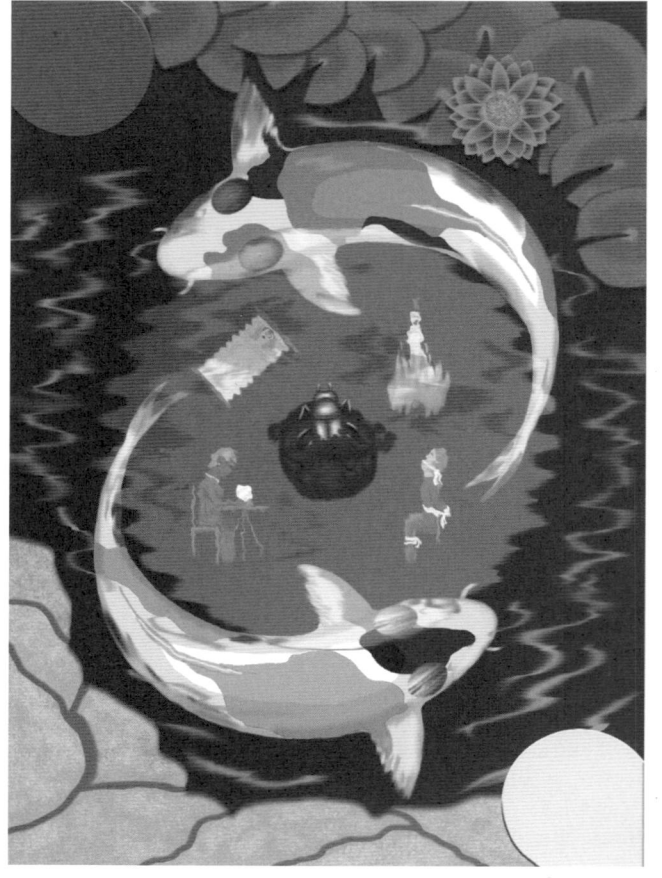

KEY PHRASES:
- The Sun is in Pisces from February 19th to March 20th.
- Twelfth sign of the Zodiac; has a natural affinity with the Twelfth House.
- Pisces is the gateway to our unconscious mind, those horrors that we imagine things to be, rather than their reality. It is our desire to avoid that which scares us, those things that we don't wish to be aware of or to see fully; therefore, its influence makes things invisible to us.
- Trying to see the truth when under the sway of Pisces is like trying to see the bottom of the ocean.
- Rules anything that is hidden, like unknown enemies, the "other" woman, your past, unidentified resources, concealed identities or motives, and family scandals; also obscured places, such as oceans, thick forests, and jungles.
- Rules the subconscious activities of the mind, like sleep, dreaming, paranoia, madness, and psychic ability.
- Rules anything that restricts or binds us—prisons, blackmail, closed systems of belief.
- Rules dark, unseen forces, such as black magic, psychic attack, and spiritual manipulation.
- Governs the feet and lymphatic system of the body. Also anything having to do with feet, such as shoes, shoe salesmen, podiatrists, wherever shoes are stored, and dancing.
- Strong affinity with the ocean and any place full of water or fish, like springs, wells, pools, pumps, rivers, and even bathtubs.
- Also rules places in which we seclude or hide our selves from the world, such as cloisters, chapels, and retreats. Rules anything with the purpose of hiding or restraining something else, like floor coverings, clouds, handcuffs, and safes.
- Rules religions, large institutions, or any group wherein the individuals become less important than "the mission." Also martyrdom or self-sacrifice for a "cause" or another person.
- Rules professions that work with liquids such as paint, alcohol, or water.
- Pisces signifies a crisis of faith or the poet's "dark night of the soul;" it is the last stage of a cold and dark winter before the light of the Sun reappears to bring warmth and illumination to our world.

UPRIGHT DIVINATORY MEANING:
The Moon upright warns the querent that she/he is not seeing something important; some truth is hidden in the matter under consideration. Something is restricting the querent. To know what is hidden or restrictive, look to the surrounding cards. Perhaps the querent is caught up in a religion of limiting beliefs, has an enemy of which she/he is unaware, or else is unaware of a family scandal or love affair that has been hidden from him or her. If well aspected, the Moon upright could suggest that the querent has considerable psychic abilities.

REVERSED DIVINATORY MEANING:
The querent is facing a crisis of faith or a "dark night of the soul." She/he fears facing the truth, wants to avoid confronting the darkness, has suppressed negative memories or moments in order to avoid experiencing the pain associated with them. Perhaps the querent is plagued with nightmares, psychically perceiving frightening energies, or else worried that his or her spouse is involved in a secret love affair. The querent may even be anxious about being trapped, arrested, or imprisoned in some way.

19 The Sun
– Sun –

Path 26: Tiphereth to Chokmah
Resh – ר : Head or face / 200 / R

Description of Illustration:

A golden-crowned, handsome king rides bareback astride a glorious lion, naked except for his royal cloak and six-rayed scepter; he smiles happily as darkness seems to run from his presence. Orbiting about his crown are all the planets of the solar system— Mercury, Venus, Earth and its Moon, Mars, Jupiter, Saturn, Uranus, Neptune, and Pluto. The Sun itself shines its approving rays down to warm him. In the distance in an ominous mirror glares a dark man who looks surprisingly like the King, only he is completely clothed and rides a black dog. UL sphere is gray (Chokmah) while LR sphere is yellow (Tiphereth).

Astrological Meaning: The Center
Element: Fire, Masculine
Rules: Leo
Minor Arcana Association: 3 Wands, 4 Pentacles, 8 Pentacles, 6 Cups, 10 Swords

Key Phrases:
- Just as the Sun of our solar system is the central life-giving force around which everything else revolves, so the Sun rules the integrity of the entire human being's system. It governs

our vitality, the amount of energy available to us, and our will to live, as well as our heart and spine. Also the right eye of men and the left eye of women.
- Wherever the Sun shines its light, it disperses the darkness.
- Rules our happiness, fun, joy, and integrity, as well as the individual's ego strength, self-worth, and self-esteem.
- Signifies royal, benevolent leadership, such as kings, heroes, and fathers.
- Sexuality of a masculine nature as well as masculinity in general.
- The Sun reveals an individual's innate talents and abilities, the direction of his or her natural development and growth, along with personal flair and style.
- Rules plants that smell pleasantly, grow majestically, and love Sunlight.
- Rules grand buildings like theatres and palaces.
- Alchemically, the Sun rules gold.

Upright Divinatory Meaning:

The Sun is always beneficial if well placed. Usually, this card suggests glory, gain, riches, and general health and vitality for the querent. The Sun shines light on the matter under consideration, illuminating the way through. When representing the querent, the Sun suggests that the querent embodies the positive, life-giving attributes of this card. It may represent a benevolent leader in the querent's life, the father, or a person whom the querent idolizes or admires; on the other hand, it may reveal information about the querent's level of bodily health, vitality, and any illnesses of the heart or spine.

Reversed Divinatory Meaning:

When reversed, the Sun suggests that the querent is "seeking the light," whether it is through immersion in enlightenment and illumination, happiness and passion, or self-esteem and self-understanding depends upon the surrounding cards. When well placed, the Sun says that the querent is either generally healthy, or else concerned with improving his or her health. If very poorly aspected, the Sun can suggest arrogance, melodramatic display, and vanity on the part of the querent, as well as worry about a subject that is ruled by the Sun.

20 The Judgment
– Pluto –

Path 30: Tiphereth to Kether
Shin – ש : Tooth / 300 / Sh

Description of Illustration:

Mighty Grecian god Hades stands sovereign in his Underworld. The Egyptian god Anubis oversees an assembly line of small earthen coal people, grasping them one by one and placing each in the fiery furnace of the planet Pluto, wherein the refuse is burned away and what is left—in all its beauty or squalor—is all that remains, even disappears, as some never make it through facing themselves fully. From the opposite side of the forge arise lovely, intricate jewel-like people—each wholly unique and individual, for all which remains after the fire of Hades is the truth. Nuit creates the ceiling of the Underworld, but now her stars have been replaced with resplendent jewels of all types and sizes. King Hades grasps the largest and most miraculous diamond in his hand, triumphant. UL sphere is white (Kether) while LR sphere is yellow (Tiphereth).

Astrological Meaning: The Transformer

Element: Fire, Androgynous
Rules: Scorpio (classical astrologers consider Pluto to share rulership with Mars)
Minor Arcana Association: Wands Suit (Fire)

Key Phrases:
- Pluto is the purifying fire that burns away all the refuse in order to bring the truth to light; it exerts tremendous pressure on the coal of our lives (and on humanity as a whole) to transform us into the diamond we're meant to be. Rules the need for change, purification, elimination, regeneration, crisis, and renewal.
- Pluto rules the Underworld, and therefore governs anything deliberately hidden, such as criminality, pornography, psychological warfare, or espionage.
- Pluto behaves amorally and unethically, thus it influences us to act without concern for rules, authority, or consequences; hence, it rules our darker urges and compulsions.
- Rules toilets, garbage, and waste. Also rules radiation—in that it burns through the cancer to bring forth new life—as well as plutonium, nuclear power, live bombs, and radiation poisoning.
- Rules the final decision, judgment, sentence, or determination of a matter without appeal in the material plane.
- Rules plutocracies, taxes, and exorbitant amounts of money (since excessive riches are rarely obtained through principled means). Rules the depravity of the mob, networks, the corporate world, insurance, and banking.
- Pluto is not so much a personal planet, as a planet of generations, mass society, and large populations. For Pluto, the progression of humanity as a whole outweighs the concerns of the individual.
- Rules the power of survival, of inevitable transformations, of beginnings and endings, of births and deaths. Rules sexual reproduction, in the sense that it is the process by which life regenerates itself and survives beyond death. Rules the sex glands, the organs of elimination, and the DNA found in cells. Also, the essential but unconscious bodily functions.

Upright Divinatory Meaning:
The querent has been placed within the crucible of fire—will she/he be consumed, or will the trial transform the canvas of his/her life into the precious gem or priceless art she/he has the potential to be? This card cautions that this is a serious situation: The querent may be about to make a large blunder. Pay attention, this is critical. An enormous change is imminent; it will be painful, but it will destroy the querent's self-made rubbish. This card reveals the final judgment or determination of a matter, without appeal in the material plane. The Judgment card may also warn us that someone is "playing with the dark" or hiding something in the situation and can't be trusted; be careful, if poorly aspected it may be warning the reader that the querent is not trustworthy and may even be dangerous.

Reversed Divinatory Meaning:
The Judgment card reversed reveals the querent's inner compulsions with which she/he is struggling. If very well aspected, it reveals the querent's struggle to transform; it shows the "hell" that he is willing to endure to achieve "heaven." If poorly aspected, it suggests that the querent is acting outside of morality or ethics; what is happening inside of the querent is so consuming that they can't trust themselves…and neither can anyone else.

21 The World
– Saturn –

Path 32: Binah to Kether
Tau – ת : Mark, Signature, Cross / 400 / Th

Description of Illustration:
Against a backdrop of three pyramids, an aged Egyptian Pharaoh presides over a council of 11 males who sit in a circle around a model-sized planet Earth. The first male is a child, and their ages get progressively older around the circle until the eleventh is almost as old as the Pharaoh; there is a twelfth chair, empty except for a pile of clothes that is stained with blood. Each member wears an elaborate headdress; the Pharaoh and the child, however, are distinctly different than the rest of the council. While the old ruler wears the crown of the god Osiris, the child wears the headdress of the god Horus. The Pharaoh and the child seem dual-natured, for they are both dark-skinned yet have brilliantly contrasting white hair and white eyebrows, as well as being clothed in white. An older woman wearing the crown of the goddess Isis stands behind the Pharaoh, clasping a black cup that seems to have captured the light. The entire group is concerned, as there are clearly some countries at war on the model Earth; the council seems to be making a decision about the hostilities on Earth. The child ceremoniously plays a black drum, emblazoned with the image of Saturn upon it, with bones for drumsticks; blood dribbles down the Pharaoh's chin. The center pyramid is engraved with the pattern of a seven circuit sacred labyrinth. UL sphere is white (Kether), while LR sphere is black (Binah).

Astrological Meaning: The Limiter

Element: Earth, Masculine

Rules: Capricorn, Aquarius (classical astrologers consider Saturn to share rulership of Aquarius with Uranus)

Minor Arcana Association: 5 Wands, 10 Wands, 7 Pentacles, 8 Cups, 3 Swords, Pentacles Suit (Earth)

Key Phrases:

- According to classical astrologers, Saturn is called the Greater Infortune or Malefic; for thousands of years this planet presided over the outermost limits of the solar system as man knew it (until the comparatively recent discovery of the three outer planets) and thus it ruled boundaries and limits (as Time is the great limiter of the human condition). The World card however, represents Saturn at his best. Saturn teaches us the cosmic lesson that as you limit yourself or are limited by outside circumstances, so will you grow.
- Saturn rules responsibility, duty, order, honor, work, discipline, and tradition.
- Rules the loss of flexibility, hardening, and weighing down of any issue; therefore, it rules old age and persistence, for as the body ages, we place the purpose of endurance as paramount and begin to fear new change and growth.
- Saturn rules governments and their resources, rules, laws, and regulations.
- Governs older men, fathers, solitary religious people, and beggars. Relates to those who work with the earth, such as farm laborers, miners, and plumbers who work with lead; also lead and lead poisoning.
- Represents world events, the Kingdom of Earth, and the physical universe; moreover, the matter under consideration and the synthesis of all the elements.
- Rules the skeleton, knees, teeth, deafness, and any illnesses caused by cold, melancholy, fears, or old age. Also the skin (as it protects us).
- Rules any location that is earthy, dirty, harsh, cold, or dark, such as deserts, deep pine forests, obscure valleys, church yards, holes, ruins, and graves; also rules places that set boundaries, like eaves, doors, fences, and thresholds.
- Alchemically, Saturn rules lead.

Upright Divinatory Meaning:

The World card represents world events, the Kingdom of Earth, and the physical universe: This card points to the crux of the matter under consideration and the synthesis of all the elements involved. If very well aspected, this card suggests that the querent has reached enlightenment in a particular realm, and so it is time to return to the rest of the world and share his or her gift(s) with the less aware. When well aspected, the World upright in a reading suggests that the querent is doing his duty—whatever the querent is doing, it will all come together. The World can also suggest that external events or world events are going to have a large impact in the querent's life. If poorly aspected, there may be a conflict with an older man or a government agency, or may indicate that the querent is avoiding doing what is appropriate in the situation. The World points the reader towards the weight of the matter.

REVERSED DIVINATORY MEANING:

The World reversed admonishes the querent that she/he needs to be more dutiful. Perhaps the querent fears aging or is resisting some limit that has been placed upon him or her. This card can also suggest that the querent is "set in his ways," inflexible, and unwilling to bend in the situation. It can also indicate that the particular subject under discussion holds great weight for the client—the greater the weight or mass, the more significance the person has attached to the matter, and the less free she/he is to act objectively/ reasonably in response. If poorly aspected, the querent may be rebelling against society, tradition, or the establishment—or may be refusing to separate his or her own significances from the truth of the matter. If very well aspected, this card can suggest that the querent desires to share his or her gifts with the world.

Kingdom Within All

No Path or Planetary Attribution
No Hebrew Letter

Ardhnarishwara, the hermaphroditic deity who is half Shiva and half Shakti, dances the cosmic dance in abandon. With legs of earth, torso of air, arms of water, and head of fire, she/he is pregnant with the yin/yang symbol. Surrounding the deity are Hadit and Nuit, the Sun and the Moon, the Fool from Trump 0 holding a joystick and Isis from Trump 21 clasping the Holy Grail. Clusters of spinning atoms and solar systems, equal in size, orbit around the god/goddess. Ardhnarishwara has removed his/her third eye from his/her forehead, and proffers the jeweled sphere to the observer as a gift, yet as we look closely at the eye, we see that it contains ever smaller versions of itself. Ardhnarishwara dances upon the white sphere of Kether at the top of the Tree of Life, while just above his/her head dangles the pendant of Malkuth.

BEYOND THE CONFINES OF ASTROLOGY:

It might seem odd to find this unique, unnumbered Major Arcana card within an otherwise conventionally structured Tarot deck; perhaps its image even vaguely reminds the reader of the traditional World (or Universe) card because of the bi-gender nature of the central figure. However, here any similarities cease.

While immersing myself in the energies of the Tarot, I eventually recognized the need for an additional card to thoroughly explore the Kingdom Within. Our modern conception of existence

has expanded exponentially since the arrangement of the Tarot deck was, for the most part, standardized, and although some Tarot creators have attempted to reinterpret the cards to allow for the vast distances traveled by the human race in past years, something always seems lost to me in attempting to merge too many factors into the established twenty-two Major Arcana cards.

The traditional World card initially depicted the Renaissance vision of the restored Soul of the World; as our conception of the solar system progressed past the belief that Saturn marked the outer limits with the earth as its center, to an emphasis upon the Vast Universe (literally one verse) with its solar systems and galaxies as an infinite whole, the World card was reinterpreted as the Universe card. Now, with the advent of quantum physics, our conception of One Grand Universe has been shattered into the model of the Multiverse, wherein simultaneous possibilities, from the infinitely immense to the illimitably microscopic, abound.

On the other hand, some might suggest that the Kingdom Within All card can be subsumed within the energy of Trump 0, the Fool. After all, the Fool represents Zero, the Qabalistic triple veil of the negative, and represents each one of us, for the Pure Fool is everything, but doesn't know it—already has everything needed, but doesn't see it. However, the Fool brings us back to the Kingdom Within the Here and Now, or Hadit, while the Kingdom Within All shows us what happens AFTER Nuit and Hadit are reunited. (Around Ardhnarishwara, the central figure on this card, you will see both the Fool from Trump 0 and Isis from Trump 21, but they are simply elements of the Kingdom Within All.)

From both an astrological and Qabalistic point of view, there IS existence outside of the confines of the zodiac and the Tree of Life, respectively. While the World (or Universe) card represents ultimate ascension both astrologically and Qabalistically, there are still those whom we have called Master…Bodhisattva…Buddha…Christos….those watchers (or referees) who have expanded upwards…downwards…inwards…outwards; who are beyond playing even the game of enlightenment itself, for they ARE the Symphony of the Spheres and the Tree of Life…the Kingdom Within All.

KEY PHRASES:

- Worlds upon worlds (universes within universes) of infinite possibility.
- Change—creation, preservation, destruction—expansion and contraction—is the only constant of the physical universe. As creator, releases all creations from obligation, giving each the freedom to be what it is. As preserver, allows life to grow and transform as it will. As destroyer, terminates without regret or malice.
- Plays whichever roles or archetypes are required to achieve a particular goal; is able to be pan-deterministic (acting to satisfy the dynamics of each and all) as well as self-deterministic (acting to satisfy one's own dynamics) as opposed to being other-determined (being determined by another's self-determinism).
- Perspicacity Incarnate: Perspicacity is usually defined as insight, wisdom, and sagacity, its antonym being dense. Literally, per-space-ity is the state of perceiving spaces within spaces, the opposite of being quagmired within the density of matter and the limitations of space (and therefore time). One is insightful, wise, and sagacious to the degree that one can perceive infinite spaces; one is slow, stupid, and dense to the degree that one is limited in perception of space.
- Holographic Universe: Every part contains the whole in its entirety. The larger the part, the clearer the image of the whole. Microcosm of the macrocosm—as above, so below. Synchronicity.
- Vibration, Frequency, and Resonance: All things in this physical universe vibrate. The rate of this vibration is called frequency. The slower the vibration, the denser the thing will appear. All things are composed of wave/particles, and may appear as either one or the other, either a wave or a particle, depending upon the subjective perspective from which the thing is viewed. The observer is just as important in determining the outcome of phenomena as the thing which is observed. When two things are vibrating at the same frequency, energy is shared between them—each affecting the other by resonance. Higher frequencies eradicate lower frequencies, and lower frequencies disorganize higher ones.
- The Actual, the Idea, the Virtue, the Purity, or the Essence—in contrast to the unending mobius of duality (right/wrong, good/bad, beautiful/ugly, etc).
- Freedom from humanity's attempts to first grasp a hold of a pleasant sensation, thought, or idea; then re-create it and make it last; eventually altering it beyond recognition until all that is left is an empty, evil imitation that allows no escape.
- Seeing the web of all the intersecting points of actuality—matter, energy, space, time, thought, idea—and acting (or plucking a particular string) in agreement with each (Hadit) and All That Is (Nuit), for the benefit of each and All That Is, from the will of each and All That Is, from a place of preference, rather than impulsion.
- Existence is a game made up of barriers, freedoms, and goals; all the games of the physical universe can be summed

up in three verbs: being, doing, and having, with the physical universe itself serving as the fundamental barrier through matter, energy, space, and time.
- Serene and spacious, silent and still, clear without distortion.
- Recognizing that the source of all illusion, pain, and suffering is denial of what is. To the degree that an individual resents, denies, or avoids the failure to achieve one's goals, he or she will experience suffering, trauma, and avidyā.
- Acknowledging Ego and the Analytical Mind as the ultimate tricksters.
- The "teacher who does not teach;" it is within the static of the teacher that learners discover their own truths reflected. Pure energy provoking energy.
- Seeing that truth vanishes, while lies persist; rather than an all-or-nothing phenomenon, truth is measured in percentages and by its applicability to circumstance. Truth is not found by holding on to anything, whether beliefs or social conditioning; witnessing with both detached clarity and internal intuition, untainted by emotionalism or fixation upon achieving or attaining a particular goal.
- Symbolically, the lemniscate, the mathematical symbol for infinity, representing the balance of opposing forces; the mobious strip, a strip of paper which is twisted and attached at both ends, forming a two dimensional surface without beginning or end; ouroboros, the circular infinity snake (or dragon) which bites its own tale, a widespread symbol among the ancients—from the Egyptians to the Mayans to the Tibetans—of both the entire zodiac as well as the continual cyclical renewal of life.

Upright Divinatory Meaning:

The Kingdom Within All beckons to the querent to focus upon progression of the spirit and eternity rather than matters of the flesh and material world with which he/she is currently transfixed. If well aspected, the querent needs to confront the issue in the spirit of play, open to the lessons to be learned in the situation, regardless of outcome. If poorly aspected, the querent is lost and adrift in the mundane problems of life and missing the infinite, focusing on ends rather than on growth. It is time to cease fixating on matters of security, relationship, family, reputation, or pleasure. Expand beyond the confines of tradition and habit. Perhaps a different game beyond that of human concerns, worldly pleasures, or redemption/enlightenment engages the querent.

Reversed Divinatory Meaning:

It is time for the querent to seek the "teacher who does not teach;" seek space in solitude and time to journey within. This "teacher" may not necessarily be in human form, but may well be found in nature, works of art and beauty, or even within the silence of one's own breath. If well aspected, this card cheers the querent onward, praising him/her for creating precisely the experience that is needed to attain what is wished, relishing the journey rather than the destination. If poorly aspected, it is time for the querent to release any persisting conclusions about one's self and the situation, approaching life without preconception, with innocence and wisdom. If very poorly aspected, the querent may erroneously believe that he or she has already attained this clarity of vision.

Notes

Notes

Chapter Two

The Court Cards

Three Basic Interpretations

There are three basic methods of interpreting the Court Cards in *The Kingdom Within Tarot*: *Level of Power*, *Sign Correspondence*, and *Actual People* in the querent's life. It is crucial in an accurate reading to interpret the Court Cards *in order* of the methods as listed above. Always implement the first method of interpretation at the initial stages of a reading, Level of Power, and then add the second, Sign Correspondence, if further information is needed with regards to the Court Card. The final method, Actual People, should only be utilized when the first two methods have been completely exhausted, and the entire spread has been laid out for consideration.

METHOD ONE: LEVEL OF POWER

The *Level of Power* addresses the amount of energy that is available to accomplish the matter at hand.

Pages: You may notice in the court cards of *The Kingdom Within Tarot* that the Pages in the deck are seated (Page of Swords), reclining (Page of Pentacles), kneeling (Page of Wands) or crouching low to the ground (Page of Cups); this is to visually depict the relative powerlessness of a Page: There's not enough behind the issue to carry it to fruition in its current stage of development.

Princes: The Princes in the deck, on the other hand, are in the act of jumping or leaping; they have a much greater level of power than the Pages, but any ventures must be completed quickly because Princes accomplish their tasks alone, with little support from others: Their power does not endure.

Queens: Because Queens represent latent, passive, concealed power, they are all standing, yet partially concealed by something: the Queen of Pentacles by a hooded cloak; the Queen of Wands by a rainbow; the Queen of Cups by the hands of her husband, Uranus; the Queen of Swords by the veil that separates this world from the afterlife. A Queen's power is formidable, but for some reason her energy is trapped, bubbling beneath the surface, waiting to give birth or manifest an undertaking. Queens often communicate a need to remain dormant in a given situation: It is prudent to wait instead of act.

Kings: Each of the Kings, in contrast, is active and riding a mighty steed that displays the characteristics akin to his suit; Kings portend enduring strength that is wholly supported to accomplish all goals. A King usually predicts great success in the endeavor under discussion.

METHOD TWO: SIGN CORRESPONDENCE

The next enlightening method of interpreting the Court Cards is their *Sign Correspondence*. Each Tarot suit has three corresponding astrological signs:

Pentacles are the **earth** signs Taurus, Virgo, and Capricorn;

Wands are the **fire** signs Aries, Leo, and Sagittarius;

Swords are **air** signs Gemini, Libra, and Aquarius;

Cups are **water** signs Cancer, Scorpio, and Pisces.

The twelve astrological signs of the zodiac are really the four elements (or states of matter) of the universe:

Fire (plasma)

Air (gas)

Water (liquid)

Earth (solid)

—combined with the three expressions of energy—

START (a scattering, dispersal, or release of energy in all directions)

CHANGE (directed flow of movement or action)

STOP (friction, opposition, or blockage)

— and the three categories of astrological signs (**Cardinal**, **Mutable**, or **Fixed**)—

The **Cardinal Signs** of the Zodiac (Aries, Cancer, Libra, and Capricorn) are goal-oriented and focused upon accomplishing a specific task through direct action or *doing, changing* energy from one point in space to another point along a straight line.

The **Mutable Signs** (Gemini, Virgo, Sagittarius, Pisces), in contrast, demonstrate a general all-directions *start* of energy either from or to a point in space; they have a rapid, constantly fluctuating viewpoint that is primarily concerned with *being*.

The final four signs, the **Fixed Signs** (Taurus, Leo, Scorpio, Aquarius), display a stubborn holding position of *having* as their energy movements conflict directly with themselves or others, forming a standing wave or mass, a *stop*.

To integrate all this information:

Pages STOP action.

Pages signify the Fixed Sign in a particular suit; thus, the Page of Pentacles is Taurus, the Page of Wands would be Leo, the Page of Swords would be Aquarius, and the Page of Cups is Scorpio: The Pages express the energy of their equivalent element by causing some sort of stop.

Princes START action.
   Princes share characteristics with the Mutable Sign in their elemental suit, combining their matching element with the energy expression of starting.

Queens and Kings CHANGE action.
   Sharing the traits of the Cardinal Sign in their elemental suit, they combine the energy of changing with the corresponding element of their suit. The difference between the action of a Queen and a King of the same suit is the DIRECTION of the change: Queens are passive, representing the *other* in the energy transaction, while Kings are active in their manifestation of the suit's energy, the *originator* of the outflow of energy.

   Thus, we discover the *method* in which energy is manifesting in our lives through the Court Cards.
   On each of the **Kingdom Within All** Court Cards, to the left of the character's name you will see the astrological symbol for the astrological sign associated with that character, and to the right you will find one of the following three symbols:

A symbol of a *solitary arrow* pointing to the *right* for a **change outwards** (or outchange) and pointing to the *left* for a **change inwards** (or inchange),

A *circle of lines* (for **start**)

An *arrow pointing towards a line* (for **stop**)

Method Three: Actual People

The final, and by far the most widespread, interpretation of the Court Cards are as *Actual People* in the querent's life:

A **Page** is generally a child or maiden.

Princes are young men (or occasionally young women), usually single, under the age of forty—a person who is actively seeking, but hasn't yet attained, a complete sense of self.

An older woman—or any woman, at any age, who has given birth—is represented by a **Queen**.

Any older man, or highly successful man, is signified by a **King**.

Each person displays the characteristics of the corresponding Tarot suit:

Wands talk about matters of creativity, desire, and power.

Pentacles discuss the resources (usually career and money) to attain one's goals.

Cups deal with the inner realms of emotion, intuition, love, and mysticism.

Swords focus on the demesnes of the mind, communication, and conflict.

For instance, the Queen of Swords might be an older, intelligent divorcee. The Page of Wands could be a precocious, creative child. If the querent has a wealthy, successful father, he would appear in the reading as the King of Pentacles, while a charming suitor who's pursuing the querent could appear as the Prince of Cups.

If the querent knows the Sun sign or ascendant from the natal chart of the important people in his or her life, this can reveal further insight. The King of Cups would be a successful older man who is emotionally mature and spiritually grounded, but if the querent knows two men who fit this description, then the one with a water sign (Cancer, Scorpio, or Pisces) for his sun sign or ascendant would be the correct individual. However, knowledge of sun signs and ascendants are not necessary, and should only be referred to when there are multiple people who seem to fit the personality of the particular Court Card.

Reversed Court Cards

If a Court Card is reversed, it does not represent an actual person in the querent's life, but instead either characterizes the energy that emanates from the querent, or else suggests that the querent is thinking of or concerned about a person whom the Court Card characterizes.

Card Analysis Classification

For each Court Card you will find the following information:

- Name of Court Card: Character
- Description of the Card's Illustration
- Archetype and its Significance
- Upright Divinatory Meaning:
- Method One: Level of Power
- Method Two: Astrological Association
- Type of Sign
- Energy of Sign
- Method Three: Actual People
- Reversed Divinatory Meaning

Archetypes

The characters associated with each of the Court Cards are symbolic archetypes drawn from the rich, fertile history of our own western myths, religions, and literature. As archetypes, each reveals an *image, ideal, or pattern that has come to be considered a universal model of humanity*. Although archetypes saturate the entire Tarot deck, we can use the sixteen archetypes of the Court Cards to help recognize *the basic patterns and roles that we naturally enact when incarnated into a physical body*. The danger of any archetype is mistakenly over-identifying with it, falsely believing that we are actually the "face" of any given archetype, rather than seeing that it is simply a role played by our spirit in order to accomplish some desired result in the material realm.

PENTACLES:

    King of Pentacles: Father Time
        Archetype: Capitalist, Authority, Destroyer

    Queen of Pentacles: Mary, the Virgin Mother
        Archetype: Channel, Queen, Pilgrim

    Prince of Pentacles: The Oak King (Holly King)
        Archetype: Critic, Martyr, Rival

    Page of Pentacles: The Newborn King
        Archetype: Eternal Child, The Rock, Epicure

WANDS:

    King of Wands: Jesus Christ
        Archetype: Hero, Wounded Healer, God

    Queen of Wands: Eostre
        Archetype: Goddess, Creator, Artist

    Prince of Wands: Dionysus
        Archetype: Philosopher, Rebel, Player

    Page of Wands: Mary Magdalene
        Archetype: Prostitute, Seductive Muse, Seeker

CUPS:

    King of Cups: The Green Man
        Archetype: Counselor, Father, Protector

    Queen of Cups: Gaia
        Archetype: Mother, Healer, Avenger

    Prince of Cups: Sir Galahad
        Archetype: Mystic, Innocent, Romantic

    Page of Cups: Faerie Puck
        Archetype: Trickster, Shape-Shifter, Spy

SWORDS:

    King of Swords: Mictlantecutli
        Archetype: Mentor, Sage, Advocate

    Queen of Swords: Hecate
        Archetype: Witch, Crone, Scapegoat

    Prince of Swords: The Lord of Misrule
        Archetype: Storyteller, Clown, Thinker

    Page of Swords: Persephone
        Archetype: Victim, Damsel, Ingénue

Minor Arcana Connection

When you begin your study of the Minor Arcana, you may notice that the characters from the Court Cards of *The Kingdom Within Tarot* pictorially play a major role in the Minor Arcana cards that correspond to his or her suit. (For example, Father Time, the King of Pentacles, is the central figure in the illustration of the Two of Pentacles.) While their involvement in the Minor Arcana often mirrors each character's actual myth, there are some Minor Arcana cards in which a character is used to portray the *meaning* of the card, rather than relate a moment from the character's own story. (For example, Hecate, the Queen of Swords, portrays the Goddess mourning the deceased God in the 3 of Swords—not a chapter from her own mythology, but vital to understanding the energy of this card and the mythological cycle story of the suit.)

Seasons and Celebrations

Also, you will probably notice while you study the Court Cards and the Minor Arcana that each Tarot suit corresponds to a particular season in the year's cycle:

> Pentacles are set in Winter
> Wands are set in Spring
> Cups are set in Summer
> Swords are set in Autumn

On the wheel of the zodiac, the sun enters the constellation of Aries (the Cardinal Fire Sign) at the start of Spring, travels through Cancer (the Cardinal Water Sign) during Midsummer, journeys through Libra (the Cardinal Air Sign) during the season of Autumn, and enters Capricorn (the Cardinal Earth Sign) in Winter; thus, each suit is set in its corresponding astrological season of the year:

Wands are fiery, a time of resurrection and rebirth as the sleeping Earth awakens and bursts forth with new life and promise;

Cups are watery, a time for the fecund Earth to present us with her bounty as we vacation, relax, and celebrate all the riches that the year has produced, heavy with our treasures;

Swords are airy, for with the coming of Autumn we face shorter days, beautiful endings in both gorgeous sunsets and multi-colored falling leaves, and the destruction of the Earth's excesses;

Pentacles are earthy, as the Sun is little with us and the Earth withdraws into herself for her winter hibernation as she awaits the returning strength of the Sun in springtime.

Within the illustrations of *The Kingdom Within Tarot* deck, the characters' mythological traditions correlate to the time-honored events and significances that represent the seasonal celebrations and customs attributed to their suit; for instance, just as Springtime focuses upon the renewal of the Sun and the Earth, so the King of Wands (Jesus Christ) and the Page of Wands (Mary Magdalene) represent central figures in the Christian celebration of Easter; meanwhile, Eostre (the Queen of Wands) is the Anglo-Saxon goddess of Springtime, and Dionysus (the Prince of Wands) represents the ancient Greek mystery cycle of resurrection and transformation.

Please Note: Since I live north of the earth's equator, the seasons of the four suits of this deck correlate to the seasons as I have experienced them during my lifetime. If you live south of the equator (such as in Australia), your seasons are opposite to those above.

The Myers-Briggs® Connection

It has also been suggested by popular writers of the Tarot that the sixteen Court Cards match up nicely to the sixteen personality types of the Myers-Briggs Type Indicator® (MBTI®) personality test. Simply put, the MBTI® (based upon the work of psychologist Carl Jung) introduces four main criteria for classifying people:

Introvert (I) vs. Extrovert (E), the source and direction of a person's energy;

Intuition (N) vs. Sensing (S), the method of information perception;

Thinking (T) vs. Feeling (F), how a person processes information; and

Perceiving (P) vs. Judging (J), how a person implements the processed information.

These criteria, in turn, produce four basic human temperaments and sixteen personality or character types. Each of the four temperaments may be assigned to a Court suit, based upon the core temperaments: SJ (Pentacles), SP (Wands), NF (Cups), and NT (Swords). Each individual Court Card represents one of the sixteen personality types as well, and its correlation is included with its description.

The Pentacles Court

King of Pentacles

— Father Time —

Description of Illustration:
    Ancient, obviously prosperous, Father Time is dressed in a toga as his beard trails to the ground; he rides an enormous, aged tortoise as he vigorously shakes a snow globe of the Earth in one hand and grasps a sickle in the other. There is a Dali-esque sprinkling of various clocks and pentacles against a snow-covered landscape and a pitch-black sky.

Archetype:
    Capitalist, Authority, Destroyer

Significance of the Archetype:
    In our contemporary New Year's celebration, Father Time is the ancient watcher of the passing hours of the old year who is replaced at midnight by the Baby New Year. This tradition, of course, is easily traceable back to the Greek god Cronos, as the Lord of Time who slowly cuts away (or kills) the hours of humanity. Old Father Time rules the material realm as he determines the lifespan of everything in it—our jobs, our possessions, our relationships, our lives, and even our world.

Upright Divinatory Meaning:

Level of Power:

The power, the support, and the resources are available for success in any financial, career, or material endeavor.

Astrological Association: Capricorn

Type of Sign: Cardinal

Energy of Sign: The King of Pentacles actively reaches outwards to the relationships, workplace, or society around him and causes others to compel him to do his duty. (outchange of doing combined with earth element)

Actual People: ESTJ

ESTJs enforce and supervise by nature; focusing their energies outwards, they are most comfortable dealing with facts, logical structures, and common sense as they build and establish reality.

An older man (probably married) who is successful in the areas of finances, career, and standing in society—perhaps a banker, government official, or any professional man. May have an earth sign (Taurus, Virgo, Capricorn) for his sun sign or ascendant.

Reversed Divinatory Meaning:

The querent either is concerned about or seeking a man who exhibits the qualities of the King of Pentacles (such as an expert in a particular profession), or else wishes to grow in the areas in which the King of Pentacles excels: finances, career, reputation, and success in the material realm. If poorly aspected, this placement either suggests that the querent needs to be more dedicated and dutiful in order to achieve his or her goals, or else that the querent considers him—or herself to be considerably more successful than is actual. Is the querent enacting the Capitalist, the Authority, the Destroyer in this situation?

Queen of Pentacles

– Mary, the Virgin Mother –

Description of Illustration:

A pregnant Mary rides on a donkey across a quiet desert towards a cave from which bright light emanates; she is wrapped in a hooded cloak that trails to the ground and seems to become the Earth beneath her. Snow-dusted mountaintops mark the horizon; a star shines above the cave, the heart of which is a pentacle.

Archetype:

Channel, Queen, Pilgrim

Significance of the Archetype:

Mary, the "Madonna" (from the Italian mi donna, "my lady"), represents the mortal (or earthly) half of Jesus Christ, who was called both the "Son of Man" and the "Son of God." In this scene, she is riding towards the cave (many scholars suggest that Jesus was actually born in a cave, as was the common place to stable animals at that time) wherein she will give birth to the baby Jesus, a blessed event that Christians celebrate as "Christ-Mass" every December 25th. ("Mass" is the Christian celebration of the Eucharist, partaking in the bread and wine as the body and blood of Christ.)

The word "virgin" in ancient Greek—the language in which the New Testament was written—was most commonly used to denote an unmarried young girl. The critical misinterpretation of the word "virgin" in Isaiah 7:14 by the Septuagint was a translator's error; the Hebrew word *almah*, denoting the social and legal status of an unmarried girl, was read as the Greek *parthenos*, which actually refers to a physiological and psychological fact. (The Hebrew word for a physical virgin is *bethulah*, not *almah*.) Parthenogenesis is the conception of a child by a female without the fertilization of mortal male seed, and was most commonly used in the Greek myths to describe the many half-god, half-human children fathered by Zeus.

In Latin, the language of Rome (wherein all the events of the Gospels take place) the word for "virgin" is *virgo*, which is best translated *young girl*; if a girl was physically a virgin she was a *virgo intacta*. The singular word *virgo* was also often used as a label of power and independence that classified those goddesses who were neither owned nor beholden to any male. Often a *virgo* was a priestess to the goddess of the harvest, Demeter, in the Mediterranean temples during the golden age of Rome.

The Virgin Mother Goddess giving birth to the Newborn God King also plays a crucial part in the winter rites of the Pagan Mystery Traditions.

Upright Divinatory Meaning:

Level of Power:

The querent has the potential for financial, career, or material success, but for some reason it is not ready to manifest. It is not yet time to give birth to the matter under consideration. Remain passive.

Astrological Association: Capricorn

Type of Sign: Cardinal

Energy of Sign: The Queen of Pentacles allows others to use her as a device to force themselves to do their duty. (outchange of doing combined with earth element)

Actual People: ISFJ

ISFJs nurture and protect; focusing their energies inwards, out of their quiet, conscientious observations of those around them they are able to offer clarity and remain grounded in the most extreme situations.

An older woman (or any mother) who is successful in the areas of finances, career, and standing in society. May have an earth sign (Taurus, Virgo, Capricorn) for her sun sign or ascendant.

Reversed Divinatory Meaning:

The querent either is concerned about or seeking a woman who exhibits the qualities of the Queen of Pentacles, or else wishes to grow in the areas in which the Queen of Pentacles excels: finances, career, reputation, and success in the material realm. If poorly aspected, the querent may be too passive or too careful in the matter under consideration. Is the querent enacting the Channel, the Queen, or the Pilgrim in this situation?

Prince of Pentacles
– The Oak King (Holly King) –

Description of Illustration:
Amongst piles of presents, the youthful Oak King jumps for joy; after critically analyzing the minutest detail of every gift that surrounds him, he has successfully opened his new crown: a wreath made from holly and mistletoe. In the distance, the Old Holly King (who looks a lot like Father Christmas) lies dead, having been slain by his successor, the Oak King. Two small birds, a Robin and a Wren, are locked in battle, and it appears that the Robin is winning. A round pentacle adorns the box from which the young Oak King has drawn forth his royal prize.

Archetype:
Critic, Martyr, Rival

Significance of the Archetype:
In Norse and Celtic mythology, the changing of the seasons is explained as a perpetual conflict between the Oak King (lord of light and the waxing year) and the Holly King (lord of darkness and the waning year). At Winter Solstice, the Oak King kills the Holly King and reigns supreme until Midsummer. The Holly King, on the other hand, is the Lord of the Winterwood who rules from Midsummer—when he kills his brother the Oak King—to Midwinter.

In the Oak King we see the image of the Green Man, Lord of the Greenwood, who represents growth and expansion, while in the Holly King we find the first Santa Claus, with his furred cloak and team of deer. The oak and the holly trees were sacred to the Druids; holly (in honor of the Holly King) and mistletoe (in honor of the Oak King) came into our modern Christmas celebrations as remembrance of this battle. Traditionally, the two kings battle for the favor of the Goddess, and although they fight as adversaries, they are really two sides of the One God.

Each king's reign represents the Earth's cycle of fertility, death, and rebirth: At Lammas, the height of the Holly King's reign, he sacrificially mates with the Great Mother, dies in her embrace, and is resurrected, while the Oak King mates, dies, and is resurrected at Beltane. This theme of the dying and resurrecting god is found in many mythological traditions, such as Osiris, Tammuz, Dionysus, Balder, and even Jesus. Vestiges of this duel can still be found in the myth of Gawain and the Green Knight from Arthurian Legend. An even older version of this myth is the battle of the Wren (associated with the Holly King) and the Robin (associated with the Oak King), who also battled twice a year—the Robin winning at Winter Solstice and the Wren winning at Midsummer.

UPRIGHT DIVINATORY MEANING:

LEVEL OF POWER:

There is substantial power available to the querent, but the support and resources are not there. The querent must act quickly with regards to the matter at hand, for the current potential for success in financial, career, or material endeavors will be brief. Odds are that anything undertaken at this time will not last.

ASTROLOGICAL ASSOCIATION: VIRGO

Type of Sign: Mutable

Energy of Sign: The Prince of Pentacles differentiates details, discerning the differences between things from all perspectives; he considers all viewpoints as he observes every aspect of something. (start of being combined with earth element)

ACTUAL PEOPLE: ISTJ

ISTJs inspect and discriminate; focusing their energies inwards, they stress clear knowledge and trust their previous experiences to supply them with the basis for reliable progress.

A younger, single male (probably in his twenties or thirties) who is still in the process of building his finances, career, and standing in society. May have an earth sign (Taurus, Virgo, Capricorn) for his sun sign or ascendant. Because the Prince of Pentacles is Virgo, and Virgo rules servants, this card may also represent an employee or a pet or animal in the querent's life (for our pets and animals serve us).

REVERSED DIVINATORY MEANING:

The querent either is concerned about or seeking a young man (or a pet) who exhibits the qualities of the Prince of Pentacles, or else wishes to grow in the areas in which the Prince of Pentacles excels: attention to details and meticulousness in material matters. If poorly aspected, the querent is being too critical and needs to gain some perspective. Is the querent enacting the Critic, the Martyr, or the Rival in this situation?

Page of Pentacles
– The Newborn King –

DESCRIPTION OF ILLUSTRATION:

A chubby, cherubic baby boy in a cradle seems to shine like the Sun. Two sheep, a black lamb, a donkey, and two angels surround him in reverence and exaltation. A round pentacle adorns the baby's cradle.

ARCHETYPE:

Eternal Child, The Rock, Epicure

SIGNIFICANCE OF THE ARCHETYPE:

All of creation praises the Eternal King! The Newborn King is an important archetype in midwinter: Not only were many dying and resurrecting gods purportedly born on December 25th—such as Horus of Egypt, Mithra of Persia, and Jesus of Christianity—but the Sun which "died" at Winter Solstice, the shortest day of the year, is afterwards "born" as the days begin to grow longer once again. The Sun, which was "dead" in the underworld during winter, must now be reborn to return or "resurrect" in the Spring. The old has died, now the new is come.

UPRIGHT DIVINATORY MEANING:

Level of Power:
There is little power, support, or resources available to the querent. The financial, career, or material matter under consideration will not materialize at this time.

Astrological Association: Taurus

Type of Sign: Fixed
Energy of Sign: The Page of Pentacles attempts to pull something towards itself out of the stops of matter. (stop of having combined with the earth element)

Actual People: ESFJ
ESFJs help and provide; focusing their energies outwards, they are encouraging and work to build security and personal harmony.

A child or young woman who is struggling to establish himself or herself in the material world; often has security issues. May have an earth sign (Taurus, Virgo, Capricorn) for his sun sign or ascendant.

Reversed Divinatory Meaning:
The querent either is concerned about or seeking a person who exhibits the qualities of the Page of Pentacles, or else is struggling with problems similar to those of the Page of Pentacles: Perhaps the querent feels insecure or else feels little hope for success with money or career. If poorly aspected, the querent may be too childlike or immature and needs to grow up before the harsher realities of life force the issue. Is the querent enacting the Eternal Child, the Rock, or the Epicure in this situation?

The Wands Court

King of Wands

— Jesus Christ —

DESCRIPTION OF ILLUSTRATION:
The glorious risen Christ King rides a fiery phoenix skywards, holding a bonfire in one hand and a scepter of power in the other, with the broken cross and conquered Underworld behind him.

ARCHETYPE:
Hero, Wounded Healer, God

SIGNIFICANCE OF THE ARCHETYPE:
The Lord Jesus Christ—the Son of Man and of God, who lived a mortal life, died on the cross (one of the oldest symbols of the intersection of the elements as well as of spiritual progression and degeneration), and defeated death as he resurrected to Eternal Life—is the perfect image for the King of Wands. Here we have the modern archetype of the resurrected Sun King, the Light of the World, who was separated from us for a time as he defeated death in the Underworld, only to return to us to light the Way.

UPRIGHT DIVINATORY MEANING:

LEVEL OF POWER:
The querent will be victorious in any matter regarding creativity, desire, or power.

Astrological Association: Aries

Type of Sign: Cardinal

Energy of Sign: The King of Wands directly outflows energy from himself or his own viewpoint to another or a different viewpoint, simple and straight. (outchange of doing combined with fire element)

Actual People: ESTP

ESTPs are adventurous entrepreneurs who make things happen; directing their energies outwards, they courageously take on challenges, solve problems, and actualize their ideas.

An older man (probably married) who is powerful, creative, and goal-oriented; perhaps he is an artist, entrepreneur, or philosopher. May have a fire sign (Aries, Leo, Sagittarius) for his sun sign or ascendant.

Reversed Divinatory Meaning:

The querent either is concerned about or seeking a man who exhibits the qualities of the King of Wands, or else wishes to grow in the areas in which the King of Wands excels: creativity, passion, and power. Perhaps the querent desires to start something new; if poorly aspected, she/he may wrestle with a nasty temper. Is the querent enacting the Hero, the Wounded Healer, or the God in this situation?

Queen of Wands
– Eostre –

DESCRIPTION OF ILLUSTRATION:
The goddess of the springtime steps out from behind a rainbow and onto a meadow, clothed in a crimson robe of sunlight. Wherever she steps, the snow melts and spring flowers burst into life. In one hand she grasps a golden wand (like a vibrant paintbrush) while the other holds a snow-white rabbit.

ARCHETYPE:
Goddess, Creator, Artist

SIGNIFICANCE OF THE ARCHETYPE:
Eostre is the Teutonic goddess of spring, fertility, and the East; her sacred month is April (once called "Eostremonth") and her coming is celebrated around the Vernal (Spring) Equinox with the ritual lighting of bonfires. She represents the creation and rebirth of life after the harsh winter months. She "paints" the Earth with new life every spring. Her symbols are the egg that represents rebirth, and the hare that represents fertility—the age-old ancestor of today's Easter bunny. In fact, most of the customs that we still celebrate every Easter—the theme of resurrection and new life, newborn chicks, decorated eggs, white bunnies, giving sweets and candies—are a result of the appropriation of the festival of Eostre by the Christian Church, which adopted the traditional celebrations and created "Easter,"

a celebration of the resurrected Christ. (Many authorities also connect the word "Easter" to Ishtar, the Sumerian goddess of love and war, whose celebration also took place at the Spring Equinox.)

Upright Divinatory Meaning:

Level of Power:

More time is necessary before the querent pursues any areas of creativity, desire, or power; the energy is considerable, but lies dormant within the querent in some crucial way. Remain passive at this time.

Astrological Association: Aries

Type of Sign: Cardinal
Energy of Sign: The Queen of Wands receives the direct energy move from another person or viewpoint, simple and straight. (inchange of doing combined with fire element)

Actual People: ISFP

ISFPs have finely tuned, aesthetic sensibilities; focused on their inner world, they excel in the fine arts and are dedicated to expressing their opinions and ideals.

An older woman (or any mother) who is powerful, creative, and goal-oriented. May have a fire sign (Aries, Leo, Sagittarius) for her sun sign or ascendant.

Reversed Divinatory Meaning:

The querent either is concerned about or seeking a woman who exhibits the qualities of the Queen of Wands, or else wishes to grow in the areas in which the Queen of Wands excels: creativity, passion, and accomplishment. Perhaps he or she is longing for passion and spark. If poorly aspected, the querent is being too passive or too careful in the matter under consideration. Is the querent enacting the Goddess, the Creator, or Artist in this situation?

Prince of Wands
– Dionysus –

Description of Illustration:

Dionysus, the "twice-born" beautiful youth that wears the horns of a bull and is crowned with serpents, springs forth from the thigh of his father, Zeus; he wields a wand made of fennel stalk and wound with ivy. In the background, a clustering grape vine grows from the smoldering ashes of the body of his mortal mother, Semele.

Archetype:

Philosopher, Rebel, Player

Significance of the Archetype:

Dionysus, the bull-horned god, is known as the Greek god of dance, poetry, song, and drama, as well as wine and intoxication; but most importantly, he is the god of sacred mysticism and the cycle of death and resurrection. He purportedly traveled the world with his intoxicated female worshippers, the maenads, whom he stimulated to ecstatic frenzies of sexuality and slaughter. The most represented god in ancient art, even Homer spoke of Dionysus as one of the "olden gods." Although Dionysus was originally a Minoan god of rebirth who emphasized the sacred feminine, the Greeks eventually adopted him as the central god of their sacred rites of Eleusis. There was constant conflict between the followers of Dionysus and the followers of Apollo—the Greek god of the Sun, prophecy, healing, and music—who tried to characterize Dionysus as a god for the young and intemperate. Nietzsche in *The Birth of Tragedy* even pointed out that Dionysus' dynamic of destruction and creation greatly contrasts with Apollo, the god of light and established forms.

Dionysus is known as the "twice-born" god, for he actually had two births. His first birth was a divine one to the goddess Persephone (or Demeter in some accounts) and the god Zeus, in a cave. Jealous Hera bid her uncles, the Titans, to attack the young Dionysus, and even though he attempted to escape by turning himself into a bull, they tore him into seven pieces and cooked him in a cauldron. After the Titans devoured six of the seven pieces, Zeus discovered them and razed them with his mighty thunderbolt. Only Dionysus' heart remained unharmed.

Dionysus was "born again," however, to the mortal woman Semele when Zeus appeared to her as a mortal and impregnated her with a potion made from the heart of Dionysus. Semele asked Zeus to reveal himself to her in his true, godly form, and she was reduced to ashes by his divine fire. Zeus saved the unborn Dionysus from his mother's ashes, and stitched the fetus into his own thigh, from which Dionysus was later born. His aunt, Ino, raised him in secret, but Dionysus had the tendency to drive ordinary mortals insane; Ino eventually went mad and ran into the ocean to kill herself, but instead, she was transformed into a sea goddess. As an adult, Dionysus journeyed to the Underworld and saved his mortal mother, Semele, taking her to Mount Olympus where she, just like her sister Io, became a goddess.

Because of his own resurrection, Dionysus became the god of both death and rebirth, the symbol of the divine spark in every human; his followers called him Lysios, "Redeemer." His sacred orgias (the Greek word for "divine rites") included dancing, singing, and prophesying through divine inspiration; ritual feasts wherein his followers symbolically ate of his flesh and drank of his blood; and ritual baths for the purpose of becoming a new creation, with the ultimate goal of each member awakening to his or her divine consciousness. Dionysus was the ever-coming god, and he was said to resurrect from the dead every year at his sacred rite at Delphi. The first Greek dramas were held in honor of Dionysus.

Upright Divinatory Meaning:

Level of Power:
The querent has the passion and power to achieve his or her goals, but the resources and support are lacking. Even if immediate action is taken, it will be a struggle for any success to endure.

Astrological Association: Sagittarius
Type of Sign: Mutable
Energy of Sign: The Prince of Wands is the purest expression of a spirit incarnated in matter; he creatively outbursts his energy in all directions from himself without consideration, order, or worry. (start of being combined with the fire element)

Actual People: ISTP
ISTPs are adaptable gamblers who can analyze and manipulate anything; they are action oriented and cannot stand to be "tied down."

A younger, single male (probably in his twenties or thirties) who is actively pursuing his goals in the areas of creation and power. May have a fire sign (Aries, Leo, Sagittarius) for his sun sign or ascendant.

REVERSED DIVINATORY MEANING:

The querent either is concerned about or seeking a young man who exhibits the qualities of the Prince of Wands, or else wishes to grow in the areas in which the Prince of Wands excels: optimism, confidence, and personal growth. If poorly aspected, the querent's happy-go-lucky and devil-may-care attitude is getting him or her into trouble. Is the querent enacting the Philosopher, Rebel, or Player in this situation?

Page of Wands
— Mary Magdalene —

DESCRIPTION OF ILLUSTRATION:

A woman in a sky blue robe and hooded black cloak kneels in front of the entrance to the empty cave that was once her Lord's tomb. A vibrant angel from above proffers a shining wand of light, which she takes from him with a tearful smile.

ARCHETYPE:

Prostitute, Seductive Muse, Seeker

SIGNIFICANCE OF THE ARCHETYPE:

Mary Magdalene is one of the most disputed characters in the New Testament. According to the Gospels, we are told that she was from a town called Magdala, near Tiberias. Jesus exorcised her of seven demons (Luke 8:2) and, after she remained with him during his death on the cross and burial in his tomb (Mark 15:40-47), she was the first to whom he appeared after his resurrection (Mark 16:9; Matthew 28:1-9).

This, however, is where the controversy of her story begins. Pope Gregory I was the first church official to equate Mary Magdalene with the "sinner" who anointed Jesus' feet with perfume in Luke 7:37-38, as well as with Mary the sister of Martha who also anoints Jesus in John 12:3. The Eastern Orthodox Church, however, insists that these are three distinct women. Most Protestants today think that Mary Magdalene was simply a prostitute

who became one of Jesus' key female followers and financial supporters.

Two Gnostic gospels discovered in 1945 amongst a collection of thirteen ancient codices and over fifty texts at Nag Hammadi in Egypt, made some startling new assertions that raise the importance of Mary Magdalene considerably. In the first, the Gospel of Mary, Jesus reveals important secret truths to Mary Magdalene, but not to Peter and the rest of the apostles; even more controversially, the Gospel of Philip suggests a more intimate view of Mary's relationship with Jesus when it records that Christ "loved Mary more" than the other disciples and kissed her often on the mouth. This—along with much speculative research concerning the myth of the Holy Grail, the Black Madonna, the French tradition of Mary Magdalene's ministry, and the Priory of Scion—has lead many to believe that Mary Magdalene was actually Jesus' wife.

Many biblical scholars have departed even further from the Christian Church's standard view by suggesting that Mary Magdalene and Mary the mother of Jesus probably served as priestesses in a Temple, either in the service of the Hebrew goddess of wisdom, *Sophia*, or in one of the many Pagan temples that proliferated in Rome at the time of Christ. Ancient pagan temples of both Old and New Testament times were populated with sacred temple "prostitutes" or *hetaerae*, who, amongst their other temple duties, used sexual intercourse as a rite of healing and spiritual transcendence, much like the Tantra of the Hindus. These scholars suggest that when Mary Magdalene was called a *hetaerae* back in the early centuries of Christianity, it was understood that she was a Temple Priestess, serving the Goddess. These same scholars assert that the term "Magdala" meant "high place" or "temple;" thus "the

Magdalene" was actually the high priestess of the temple. When Mary anoints Jesus in the Gospels, it might have been a reenactment of the fertility rites of the ancient Middle East. In pouring the expensive perfume over the head of Jesus, "the Magdalene" would be performing the *heiros gamos*: the ceremonial anointing of the God King for the rite of "sacred marriage" between the representatives of the God and the Goddess. Even Mary's experiences at the tomb of Jesus reflect the pagan rituals surrounding the ancient myths, when the Goddess goes to the tomb in the garden to lament the death of her Bridegroom, but instead rejoices when she finds that he has resurrected.

No matter how the individual understands Mary Magdalene's role in the life of Jesus, she is a central character in the Gospel story of his ministry and resurrection.

UPRIGHT DIVINATORY MEANING:

LEVEL OF POWER:

Any matter involving creativity, passion, or power will fail at this time; the querent currently lacks what it takes to succeed. It is not yet the querent's time.

ASTROLOGICAL ASSOCIATION: LEO

Type of Sign: Fixed

Energy of Sign: The Page of Wands strongly outflows energy from himself or herself, only to be met with an equally strong outflow from the other or others; whether this stop manifests as attention or opposition, this makes the Page more solid. (stop of having combined with the fire element)

ACTUAL PEOPLE: ESFP

ESFPs are performers and entertainers; playful and fun-loving, they enjoy pleasureful experiences, luxuriate in arousal, and live life to the fullest.

A young person who is struggling to express himself or herself in the areas of creativity, passion, or power; often this person is fixated upon seeking pleasure. May have a fire sign (Aries, Leo, or Sagittarius) for his or her sun sign or ascendant.

REVERSED DIVINATORY MEANING:

The querent either is concerned about or seeking a person who exhibits the qualities of the Page of Wands, or else is struggling with problems similar to those of the Page of Wands. If poorly aspected, the querent is fixated on seeking pleasure or else feels creatively stagnant or powerless. On the other hand, the querent may simply need attention and want to be noticed. Is the querent enacting the Prostitute, Seductive Muse, or Seeker in this situation?

The Cups Court

King of Cups
– The Green Man –

Description of Illustration:
We see the wild Lord of Nature, with his proud stag's antlers, riding a splendid seahorse through the mighty waves towards a thickly forested shore; his face seems covered with leaves, and as he raises a large oak cup in one hand, a geyser erupts from his other hand. He shines like the Sun, and it seems that his image is reflected in every aspect of the forest and sea that surrounds him.

Archetype:
Counselor, Father, Protector

Significance of the Archetype:
Decorating the churches and cathedrals of Europe, as well as many pre-Christian pagan temples and graves, is the unusual carving of a human head within a mass of leaves: the "Green Man." In Medieval times he was called "Jack in the Green," "Green Jack," or "Green George," and was associated with the original myths of Robin Goodfellow, Puck, and Robin Hood, an ancient Lord of Misrule known as the "Lord of the Merry Greenwood." The Green Man danced ahead of the Medieval May Queen in May Day pageants, a yearly celebration based upon the Christianization of ancient pagan spring fertility rites, still replete with hidden sexual images such as the phallic "maypole."

To the ancient Celts, he was the god of fertility, nature, and the underworld; they called him "Cernunnos," "Herne," or "The Horned One," and depicted him with the antlers of a stag. An ancient Sun god, he ruled the changing of the seasons. He was born at the winter solstice, married the goddess at Beltane (May 1st), and died at the summer solstice, wherein he ruled the underworld until his rebirth at the winter solstice; many scholars believe that his horned image was later merged with that of the Greek god Pan to create the common visual representation of the Devil for the Christian religion. The English epic poem Gawain and The Green Knight is a literary retelling of the Green Man, who yearly dies and is reborn.

Upright Divinatory Meaning:

Level of Power:
Success is imminent in the areas of emotion, intuition, love, and spirituality.

Astrological Association: Cancer
Type of Sign: Cardinal
Energy of Sign: The King of Cups has the unique skill of pulling the whole universe towards himself, affording him remarkable emotive and intuitive abilities when dealing with others. (outchange of doing combined with water element)

Actual People: ENFJ

ENFJs are teachers and counselors; they are most concerned with harmonious human relationships and make charismatic and successful group facilitators.

An older man (probably married) who is successful in the areas of emotion, intuition, love, and spirituality; perhaps he is a psychologist, a minister, or a nurturing husband and father. May have a water sign (Cancer, Scorpio, Pisces) for his sun sign or ascendant.

Reversed Divinatory Meaning:

The querent either is concerned about or seeking a man who exhibits the qualities of the King of Cups, or else wishes to grow in the areas in which the King of Cups excels: emotion, intuition, love, and spirituality. Perhaps the querent wants to see a psychologist, longs for a family, or desires to purchase a new home. Is the querent enacting the Counselor, Father, or Protector in this situation?

Queen of Cups

– Gaia, Mother Earth –

Description of Illustration:

A long-haired, pregnant woman whose belly is the Earth, cradles the Earth with one hand while the other pours from a lovely goblet a waterfall of water upon her rounded stomach, which becomes the ocean. The Oracle at Delphi is her navel. The vast Sky, Uranus, who is both her husband and the father of her children, surrounds and embraces her, his stars twinkling with delight.

Archetype:

Mother, Healer, Avenger

Significance of the Archetype:

The Greek philosopher, Plato, wrote that the world is in fact one living organism that possesses a psyche, or soul, and that all the individual souls of humanity are but fragments of this One Soul. The Romans called this the *Anima Mundi*, or World Soul.

According to the ancient Greeks, out of Chaos arose Gaia (or Ge), our bountiful Mother Earth. In some accounts she was a mystical egg from which Eros (Love) hatched, while in others she divided the sea from the sky in order to find a place to dance. From herself she created Uranus, the Starry Heavens. She married Uranus and gave birth to a race of giants, called "Titans," as well as to all living creatures. Uranus was continuously unfaithful, so she helped her youngest son, the Titan Cronos, rebel against his father and banish him to the distant heavens where he has since had little effect upon the affairs of this world; thus, Cronos became supreme ruler. Gaia transferred most of her previous responsibilities to her daughter Rhea, the wife of Cronos, and the other goddesses.

Eventually, Rhea, grieved that her husband, Cronos, had swallowed their first five children in order to prevent one of them from usurping his throne as he had usurped his father's, turned to her mother for help in deposing him. Gaia helped hide their sixth child, Zeus, who ultimately grew up to overthrow his father and become the great Sky God of Mount Olympus. Gaia prophesied through the Pythia at the Oracle of Delphi, the navel of the world, until she finally turned this sacred space over into Apollo's keeping. An earlier account calls her Eurynome, the "Goddess of All Things."

The influence of Gaia still permeates our modern culture. Even today, we speak of "Mother Earth" or "Mother Nature." The prefix "ge" in the words "geology" and "geography" is taken from the Greek word for earth. In the 1960s, the scientist, James Lovelock, proposed The Gaia Hypothesis, which states that our planet actually functions as a single organism that maintains the conditions necessary for its own survival. Some may question calling the Queen of Cups (the Water element) after Mother Earth, but remember—scientists estimate that 70-80% of the Earth's surface is, in fact, water.

UPRIGHT DIVINATORY MEANING:

LEVEL OF POWER:

Growing within the querent are potent emotions, intuition, love, and spirituality, but it is not yet time to release them upon the matter at hand. Be passive.

ASTROLOGICAL ASSOCIATION: CANCER

Type of Sign: Cardinal

Energy of Sign: The Queen of Cups passively allows herself to be pulled towards another with the rest of the universe; this ability makes her incredibly reflective and empathetic (as well as often psychic) in response to the energies of others. (inchange combined with water element)

ACTUAL PEOPLE: INFJ

INFJs are inspirational and insightful; with an uncanny understanding of the complexities within and between people, they are the poets, the mystics, and the martyrs of this world.

An older woman (or any mother) who is successful in the areas of emotion, intuition, love, and spirituality. Often the Queen of Cups signifies a born psychic. May have a water sign (Cancer, Scorpio, Pisces) for her sun sign or ascendant.

REVERSED DIVINATORY MEANING:

The querent either is concerned about or seeking a woman who exhibits the qualities of the Queen of Cups, or else wishes to grow in the areas in which the Queen of Cups excels: emotion, intuition, love, and spirituality. If poorly aspected, querent may be too passive or too careful in the matter under consideration; on the other hand, the querent might have latent psychic abilities that are starting to surface. Is the querent enacting the Mother, Healer, or Avenger in this situation?

Prince of Cups

— Sir Galahad —

Description of Illustration:

Crying out his fateful words, "If I lose myself, I save myself," the chivalrous knight, Sir Galahad, clad in white armor, springs forth into the air out of Merlin's chair in King Arthur's Hall, grasping for the shining image of the Holy Grail that floats elusively just out of reach above the legendary Round Table of Camelot.

Archetype:

Mystic, Innocent, Romantic

Significance of the Archetype:

The Quest for the Holy Grail is an archetypal hero's journey that is responsible for the symbol of the Cups Suit; Sir Galahad is the true Prince of Cups who finds the Holy Grail and, without undergoing physical death, enters the "spiritual city" because of his willingness to die to himself, or "lose himself." In Luke 9:24 Jesus said, "For those who want to save their life will lose it, and those who lose their life for my sake will save it." Reminiscent of the biblical characters Enoch and Elijah who also ascended to heaven without dying, Galahad's story is that of the being who has never lost his state of perfection and wholeness by believing the lies of the World of Matter and his own ego.

Most of Arthur's knights did not return from their Quest. Lancelot and Gawain returned, but had failed. Percival and Bors found the Grail, but did not return with it. Only Galahad succeeded in finding the Grail and entering the "spiritual city," never to be seen on the Kingdom of Earth again.

Upright Divinatory Meaning:

Level of Power:

The querent has the ability to succeed in the realms of emotions, intuition, love, and spirituality, but lacks the support or resources. Immediate, decisive action is needed, but if the matter is not conquered quickly then the possibility for success will dissipate.

Astrological Association: Pisces

Type of Sign: Mutable
Energy of Sign: The Prince of Cups receives energy into himself from all directions; he identifies with everyone and everything to the point of losing himself. (Start of being combined with water element)

Actual People: INFP

INFPs are the dreamers and healers of this world; their ideals and beliefs are paramount to them and their work must have meaning or they escape into fantasy to compensate.

A younger, single male (probably in his twenties or thirties) who is still in the process of pursuing and establishing his emotions, intuition, love relationships, and spirituality. If poorly aspected, the Prince of Cups may be a charmer who enchants the querent with empty praises and promises. May have a water sign (Cancer, Scorpio, Pisces) for his Sun sign or ascendant.

Reversed Divinatory Meaning:

The querent either is concerned about or seeking a young man who exhibits the qualities of the Prince of Cups, or else wishes to grow in the areas in which the Prince of Cups excels: romance, imagination, and empathy. Perhaps the querent desires to woo a new love, or else wants to take up a spiritual pursuit. Is the querent enacting the Mystic, Innocent, or Romantic in this situation?

Page of Cups

– Faerie Puck –

DESCRIPTION OF ILLUSTRATION:
The small, mischievous hobgoblin from Shakespeare's *A Midsummer Night's Dream* crouches next to a pair of sleeping lovers, cup of magic potion in hand.

ARCHETYPE:
Trickster, Shape-Shifter, Spy

SIGNIFICANCE OF THE ARCHETYPE:
The mischievous troublemaker "Puck," or "Robin Goodfellow," was one of the most popular imps in English Folklore. He was the naughty shape-shifting hobgoblin who would assume the "innocent" shapes of animals and children in order to fool humans and was blamed for sundry nuisances, such as spoons missing and travelers losing their way. His name comes from the Medieval Welsh word for the devil, "Pwca," commonly pronounced "Pooka." He's been pictured as everything from a hairy brownie, to the Greek god Pan, to an innocent, elf-like child. Immortalized in Shakespeare's *A Midsummer Night's Dream* as the madcap servant of Oberon, the Lord of the Faeries, Puck's well-intentioned mistake of giving the wrong young man a love potion provides the conflict of the comedy. Traces of his memory can be found in our culture today, from the invisible

"pooka" in the classic play and film starring Jimmy Stewart, Harvey, to the tenth moon of Uranus being named "Puck."

Upright Divinatory Meaning:

Level of Power:

Any plans or desires in the areas of emotions, intuition, love, or spirituality will not work out: the essential elements are lacking.

Astrological Association: Scorpio

Type of Sign: Fixed

Energy of Sign: The Page of Cups creates his or her own stop, for while trying to communicate, she/he simultaneously holds something back; the Page shields his or her thoughts, desires, and intentions from others. (Stop of having combined with water element)

Actual People: ENFP

ENFPs are the champions and experimenters; they constantly initiate change and focus on possibilities, avoiding the past with its consequences.

A child or young woman who is struggling with his or her emotions, intuition, love relationships, and spirituality; generally, the person is engrossed with avoiding pain. The individual may be spiritually immature, with fanatical tendencies, or conversely may be amassing too much debt. May have a water sign (Cancer, Scorpio, Pisces) for his or her sun sign or ascendant.

Reversed Divinatory Meaning:

The querent either is concerned about or seeking a person who exhibits the qualities of the Page of Cups, or else is struggling with problems similar to those of the Page of Cups: The querent may be repressing strong feelings, or might feel helpless in attaining a love relationship. If poorly aspected, the querent wishes to avoid pain at all costs, instead choosing to hide in secrets; the querent may also be worried about debt. This card sometimes indicates a basic immature (even fanatical) spiritual tendency in the querent. This person has no problem pointing out the limitations of another, but desperately hides the truth of his or her own lack. Is the querent enacting the Trickster, Shape shifter, or Spy in this situation?

The Swords Court

King of Swords

— Mictlantecutli —

Description of Illustration:
Mictlantecutli, the Aztec god of death and the underworld, flies through the skies on the back of a gargantuan bat in horrific abandon, celebrating the night when the veil between the living and the dead is at its thinnest. From one hand springs a large tornado of spiders, skeletons, tombs, jack-o'-lanterns, and autumn leaves, while his other hand grasps a great and terrible sword that drips blood. In the distance, Mexican families gather around candlelit adorned gravesites in a cemetery during Dias de Muertos to honor their deceased loved ones and the Lord of Death himself.

Archetype:
Mentor, Sage, Advocate

Significance of the Archetype:
Before the coming of the Catholic Spaniards, the indigenous Mexicans considered death and life as an opposite yet complementary duality: In order to embrace life, you must also embrace death. (Even Coatlicue, the Aztec goddess of life and the earth, was pictured wearing a death mask) Mictlantecutli, the Aztec god of the dead, was the ruler of Mictlan, the lowest layer of the Aztec underworld, located in the desolate reaches of the far north. Also called Tlalxicco, the "Navel of the Earth," he ruled his realm with his dreaded queen Mictecacihuatl; his symbolic animals were the

bat, the owl, and the spider. He was generally pictured as a huge skeleton with hands and feet made of flesh, or else wearing a huge skull with a gaping maw that ate the spirits of those who were unfit to enter the paradise of Tlaloc because they had not died honorably in battle, by drowning, or in childbirth. Since humans were ritually sacrificed to Mictlantecutli, he was also often portrayed with a bloodied sacrificial knife or sword. Mictlantecutli's message to the Aztecs and their descendants was an important one: The significance of a life is not determined by how one lives, but by how one dies.

Uniting pre-Columbian practices with the syncretism of the Dominican missionaries, an entirely new form of Catholicism emerged in Mexico. In numerous cultures, October 31st is considered to be the day that the veil between the world of the living and the world of the dead is at its thinnest, but Mexico celebrates this event distinctively. October 31st through November 2nd is the holiday of Dias de Muertos, the perfect example of the blending of Aztec and Catholic belief systems. The week prior is spent in busy preparations, as each family builds a fragrant altar made of sugarcane and marigolds, called an ofrenda, covering it with various foods, offerings, and mementos for their deceased. During the actual event, they travel to the village cemetery and decorate the graves of their dearly departed, sitting and communing with them as they share their bounty with their ancestors, celebrating and remembering those who have come before.

The image of Mictlantecutli is everywhere during Dias de Muertos: From the decorated shop windows to the folk art and children's costumes, you find hordes of skeletons celebrating gleefully. With the help of the satirical illustrators Manilla and Posada, the danse macabre or "dance of death" (artistically depicted skeletons dancing and playing musical instruments) of a plague-riddled Medieval Europe made its way into the Mexican customs and folk art of this holiday in the form of las calaveras, literally "skulls;" these calaveras are either sugar skulls with the name of a deceased stamped on its forehead, sculptured or drawn cartoonish scenes of merrymaking skeletons, or satirical poems that all have one purpose: to celebrate the Mexican's view of the reciprocity of death and life. Whether venerated or feared, Death walks by our side—so why not be amigos? In present-day Mexican folk art, the personified Death is sometimes called Santa Muerte, "Saint Death" and is depicted as a white-robed skeleton. Other times personified as a female—La Calaca or La Muerte—death incarnate stands robed like a saint and holds a scythe, an owl, and an hourglass; even a cartoonish version of death dressed as an elegant lady, the famous Catrina, is an artistic image that was popularized by the artists Posada and Rivera.

Mictlantecutli, the Skeleton King himself, reminds us of the important truth that Dias de Muertos celebrates: To be born is only to begin to die.

Upright Divinatory Meaning:

Level of Power:

The querent will win in matters pertaining to the mind, communication, or conflict.

Astrological Association: Libra

Type of Sign: Cardinal

Energy of Sign: The King of Swords mentally reaches out to perceive both sides of any directly opposing issue; his agile mind perceives far more because of his awareness of multiple viewpoints. (outchange of doing combined with the air element)

Actual People: ENTP

ENTPs are the innovators and inventors; striving for a balanced and just world, they are able to both successfully mediate change as well as challenge and improve the status quo.

An older man (probably married or recently divorced) who excels at mental activities, communication, and winning conflicts; perhaps he is a lawyer, a journalist, or a teacher. May have an air sign (Gemini, Libra, Aquarius) for his sun sign or ascendant.

Reversed Divinatory Meaning:

The querent either is concerned about or seeking a man who exhibits the qualities of the King of Swords, or else wishes to grow in the areas in which the King of Swords excels: knowledge, wisdom, and winning conflicts. The querent may be worried about matters of partnership. Is the querent enacting the Mentor, Sage, or Advocate in this situation?

Queen of Swords
– Hecate –

Description of Illustration:
The Crone stands at the crossroads before a large cauldron; she uses one hand to stir the churning waters with a frightening sword, while with the other she pulls aside the thin veil that separates this world from the afterlife to gaze directly at us; her formidable stare seems to pierce right through us, deftly judging our worth. Simultaneously, she cries great tears that fall into her cauldron; within the cauldron's murky depths we can just make out the distant image of her lost beloved, the Lord of the Shadows. Small spirits of the deceased are returning to her cauldron to reincarnate. Above her a pack of hounds bay at the waning moon that is partially covered by clouds.

Archetype:
Witch, Crone, Scapegoat

Significance of the Archetype:
Hecate is a multifaceted goddess. Known as the Greek goddess of the dark moon, the night, midwifery, the crossroads, and the underworld, she was called the "far-seeing" goddess, for she had the ability to see in all directions, even the past, present, and future. Because of this unique ability, she was usually depicted with some version of three heads: either a beautiful woman with three human heads (one a maiden, one a mother, and one an old

woman); three animal heads (one snake, one horse, and one boar); or else she traveled with a three-headed black hound. At night during the dark moon, Hecate walked the roads of Greece with her howling hounds, visiting cemeteries and leading shades to the underworld. The daughter of Titans, Zeus shared with Hecate—and only Hecate—the power to grant (or refuse to grant) the wishes of humanity.

As time progressed, greater focus was placed on Hecate's knowledge of the darker, natural mysteries, and she began to be pictured as a "hag" or a "crone," eventually given the title "Queen of the Witches." During the Middle Ages and the Renaissance, the Catholic Church blamed Hecate (and all "witches") for many unexplained "evil" events; even in Shakespeare's *Macbeth*, she is characterized as the evil goddess of the witches. Instead of embodying the three-faced triple goddess within herself, she eventually assumed the last aspect of the triple goddess, with Persephone (or Artemis, or Kore) as the maiden aspect and Demeter (or Selene) as the mother aspect. Regardless, it is she who helps make transitions and reveals the power of the darkness and shadows.

UPRIGHT DIVINATORY MEANING:

LEVEL OF POWER:

The Queen of Swords slashes with her mighty sword to sway the scales and upset the current balance of things: Something is about to end in the querent's life. To identify what is ending, look to the surrounding cards. The querent contains considerable mental resources to succeed in the realms of a communication or a conflict, but the external circumstances are such that now is not the time to act. Wait until things settle down a bit.

ASTROLOGICAL ASSOCIATION: LIBRA

Type of Sign: Cardinal

Energy of Sign: The Queen of Swords allows the other to fully see her own perspective, immersing the other in the "logical correctness" of the Queen's experience. (inchange of doing combined with the air element)

ACTUAL PEOPLE: INTP

INTPs are both architects and magicians; they love intellectual problems and seek to understand and manipulate the people and phenomena around them.

An older woman (or any mother) who excels at mental activities, communication, and handling conflict—also represents a divorcee. May have an air sign (Gemini, Libra, Aquarius) for his Sun sign or ascendant.

REVERSED DIVINATORY MEANING:

The querent either is concerned about or seeking a woman who exhibits the qualities of the Queen of Swords, or else wishes to grow in the areas in which the Queen of Swords excels: intelligence, communication, and conflict. Perhaps the querent wants something to end or fears something ending, like a marriage or a job. To know what the querent wishes to end, look to the surrounding cards. Is the querent enacting the Witch, Crone, or Scapegoat in this situation?

Prince of Swords
– THE LORD OF MISRULE –

DESCRIPTION OF ILLUSTRATION:
A Medieval court jester dances and laughs, carelessly juggling a coffin, a skull, and a deadly-looking sword as he bounds through the air, showing us that we should never take death too seriously.

ARCHETYPE:
Storyteller, Clown, Thinker

SIGNIFICANCE OF THE ARCHETYPE:
The Lord of Misrule (also called the Abbot of the Revels) was the elected master of the winter celebrations in Medieval Europe. The peasants would draw lots, and the winner generally began his topsy-turvy reign on All Hallow's Eve and ruled throughout the Christmas season. Wearing a paper crown and the jester's motley, the Lord of Misrule turned everything "upside down," as the ruling noble gave him full license to imbue the holiday season with whatever naughty decadence that he might wish. This tradition can be traced back to the ancient Saturnalia, the Roman celebration of the rebirth of the Sun. During this festival of role-reversals, servants were given equality with their masters and a commoner was chosen as King of the Festival, impersonating Saturn and being treated as royalty throughout the celebration until he was sacrificed on the altar of Saturn at the

close of the festival! The Lord of Misrule reminds us to fully enjoy every moment and stop taking life (and death) so seriously.

Upright Divinatory Meaning:

Level of Power:

The querent has substantial abilities in matters of the mind, communication, or a conflict, but little or no support to succeed. Immediate action garners the only possibility of success; the longer it takes, the greater the chance of failure. The Prince of Swords may also bring an important message or communication into the querent's life.

Astrological Association: Gemini

Type of Sign: Mutable
Energy of Sign: The Prince of Swords maintains a comfortable, detached distance from everyone and everything, rationally emphasizing all the similarities and generalities of experience; he never dirties himself with the depths of specifics or contradiction. (Start of being combined with air element)

Actual People: INTJ

INTJs are free-thinkers and masterminds; ingenious by nature, they stretch and play with ideas and conventions like taffy.

A younger, single male (probably in his twenties or thirties) who is busily developing his intellect, communication skills, and ability to win conflicts. Because the Prince of Swords corresponds to Gemini, this person may have an important message for the querent, or, if poorly aspected, may be a spy or informant. May have an air sign (Gemini, Libra, Aquarius) for his Sun sign or ascendant.

Reversed Divinatory Meaning:

The querent either is concerned about or seeking a young man who exhibits the qualities of the Prince of Swords, or else wishes to grow in the areas in which the Prince of Swords excels: cleverness, adaptability, and the ability to see the similarities and relationships between things. Perhaps the querent wants to return to school or is concerned about the proper credentials or paperwork to accomplish his or her goals. If poorly aspected, this card in the reversed position also suggests that the querent is only looking at the superficial, surface details of the issue. Is the querent enacting the Story-teller, Clown, or Thinker in this situation?

Page of Swords

– Persephone –

DESCRIPTION OF ILLUSTRATION:
Holding a pomegranate with a bite taken out of it in one hand and a collapsed sword in the other, both lovely and horrible, Persephone sits sorrowfully enthroned in the foreground; one half of the landscape behind her is covered in winter while the other half of the landscape is covered in spring.

ARCHETYPE:
Victim, Damsel, Ingénue

SIGNIFICANCE OF THE ARCHETYPE:
Persephone was the Greek goddess of the spring and daughter of Ceres, the goddess of the harvest, until the Lord of the Underworld, Hades, decided he wanted her. With the help of his brother, Zeus, Hades kidnapped Persephone and carried her down to his dark realm. The Earth became barren as Ceres grieved the loss of her daughter. As Earth experienced its first winter and humanity and all Earth's inhabitants began to starve, Zeus finally commanded his brother to return Persephone to her mother; clever Hades, however, tricked Persephone into eating in the Underworld by taking one single bite of a pomegranate, and since it was decreed that anyone who eats in the Underworld must live there, Persephone was doomed to live six months in the Underworld with Hades and six months on the surface with her mother, never quite fitting

into either realm. Persephone became the Dark Mistress of the Underworld, as well as the maiden of the waxing new moon who rules the changing of the seasons.

In Greek mythology, Persephone shares her rulership of the Underworld with Hecate, the Queen of Swords in *The Kingdom Within Tarot*. Both goddesses also represent opposite phases of the moon—Persephone the new moon and Hecate the full moon. While it is easy to relate Persephone with the classical image of the Queen of Swords that appears in most decks, she is the Page in *The Kingdom Within Tarot* for good reason: In Persephone we have the maiden forced to grow up before she is ready, the victim who has not yet accepted responsibility for her own life, the damsel who pines for her dreams of perfection yet seems unable to achieve them. Hecate, on the other hand, chooses to rule the Underworld as a result of her Wisdom and Mastery of the Darkness. Persephone must learn to balance the extremes of her ideals with the bitter realities of life before truly realizing her own power—one of the first lessons of all who would call themselves "human."

UPRIGHT DIVINATORY MEANING:

LEVEL OF POWER:

The situation contains too many conflictive elements that work against each other; the matter will come to little.

ASTROLOGICAL ASSOCIATION: AQUARIUS

Type of Sign: Fixed

Energy of Sign: The Page of Swords watches as she induces others to stop against themselves in reaction to her own dynamic expressions of freedom; when others stop around her, the Page successfully gains more space to be creative and original. (Stop of having combined with air element)

ACTUAL PEOPLE: ENTJ

ENTJs are best at motivating others to grow to new heights; they logically apply their ideals to improve and create their conceptions of a "brave new world."

A child or young woman who has an important message but is struggling with how to logically communicate it amidst opposing forces. May be brilliant and argumentative by nature; struggles with issues of purpose and self-identity. May have an air sign (Gemini, Libra, Aquarius) for his or her sun sign or ascendant.

REVERSED DIVINATORY MEANING:

The querent either is concerned about or seeking a person who exhibits the qualities of the Page of Swords, or else is struggling with problems similar to those of the Page of Swords: Perhaps the querent feels lost and without purpose. The querent may be upset over feelings of not fitting in while at the same time not feeling free. Perhaps she is waiting for someone to save her from the current situation or herself. Is the querent enacting the Victim, Damsel, or Ingénue in this situation?

Notes

Notes

Notes

Chapter Three

The Minor Arcana

The Pentacles Suit

Ace of Pentacles

Root of Earth / Kether of Assiah

Description of Illustration:
The card is filled with the image of the planet Earth. Superimposed upon the Earth is a huge hand that holds up a large engraved pentacle. Floating above we see an Earthy Crown. A white sphere (Kether) peeks over the bottom center edge of the card.

Key Phrase:
Power of Earth

Upright Meaning:
The promise of success in any material endeavor is at hand, whether in finances, career, or physical happiness: Now is the time to begin. This card can also warn the querent to protect him—or her—self in the physical realm.

Reversed Meaning:
The querent contains all the desire, possibilities, and power necessary for success, but they lie dormant within the querent, unable or unwilling to manifest as of yet. The querent's attention is captured by the possibility of solid accomplishment.

Two of Pentacles

Jupiter in Capricorn (Fall) / Chokmah of Assiah

Description of Illustration:
In the foreground, Father Time is balancing two pentacles, one in each hand—it looks like the higher one might almost fall. A goat balances on the planet Jupiter in the snow-covered background. A gray sphere (Chokmah) peeks over the bottom center edge of the card.

Key Phrase:
Successful Change

Upright Meaning:
Successful change in the material realm, but to the detriment of spiritual progression. Career and finances will improve; the querent will win the court case or the promotion—even though she/he may not deserve it. If poorly aspected, forceful control is required in order to resolve a difficult situation. A sensitive consideration of the aesthetics of the situation is needed.

Reversed Meaning:
If the querent does what the surrounding cards demand, then the situation will improve. The querent may be rigidly orthodox, moral, austere, and ambitious to a fault, driven by the desire for prominence. This card in the reversed position indicates that there is a need for the querent to accept full responsibility for his or her

position and exert control in order for the situation to improve; it may also indicate that the querent is seeking a harmonious change to the circumstances, but what underlies this wish is a desire to further his or her own situation. Querents with this card reversed are using the respect of others to prove their own value to themselves, hence their spirituality rests upon the authority that is granted to them by others.

Three of Pentacles

Mars in Capricorn (Exaltation) / Binah of Assiah

Description of Illustration:

The Oak King hammers diligently as he builds himself a throne; the throne stands on a dais in front of a huge stained-glass window whose image is three pentacles forming a triangle with the planet Mars at the center. It is snowing, and a goat holds the nails for the Oak King in his mouth. A black sphere (Binah) peeks over the bottom center edge of the card.

Key Phrase:

Triumph After Toil

Upright Meaning:

Success in the material realm as a result of hard work; opportunities for success are approaching—don't miss them. The work that the querent is doing or is thinking about having done is worthwhile, but it will not be easy. The querent will not like the judge's judgment in a court case, but it's best for everyone.

Reversed Meaning:

The querent is driven by the desire for power and authority, but frustrated by the restrictions to his or her success. She/he may be lonely at work and burdened by heavy responsibility, perhaps even working with undependable people. Disinterest complicates the querent's struggle.

Four of Pentacles

Sun in Capricorn / Chesed of Assiah

Description of Illustration:
The long night is broken as the Sun shines (with an image of the Newborn King within it) above the barren, snow-covered landscape (which looks remarkably like a sleeping woman). A ray of sunshine, like a shower of golden coins interspersed with four pentacles, pours forth upon the ground, melting the snow as a cheery sunflower sprouts upwards beneath its warmth. A goat lies next to the flower, protecting it from harm. A blue sphere (Chesed) peeks over the bottom center edge of the card.

Key Phrase:
Acquisition

Upright Meaning:
When upright and well aspected, this card promises material attainment and power as well as stabilization of finances and career; the querent may receive special recognition or the assistance of an influential person in some way. If poorly aspected, this card suggests that the querent is (greedily) holding on much too tightly to material acquisitions—she/he must RELEASE the grip for prosperity to flow. Covert hostility complicates the matter.

REVERSED MEANING:

The querent is dissatisfied with his or her current situation, and has designs to find or create material wealth; if poorly aspected, this can suggest that the querent is pretending she/he has more (or is more) than is actual, indicating excessive spending on the querent's part as though wealthier than she/he actually is. Finally, the querent may be aiming beyond his or her reach, using acquisition of resources to prove personal power and worth.

Five of Pentacles

Mercury in Taurus / Geburah of Assiah

Description of Illustration:

Mary clasps the toddler, Jesus, to her breast as she crouches in fear upon the back of a bull lead by her husband, Joseph; they are fleeing to Egypt to escape from Herod's soldiers who search to destroy their son. Five pentacles trail behind them in the snow, as if they lost five coins in their flight. Joseph grasps the planet Mercury in his hand, looking at it as though consulting a compass for direction. A red sphere (Geburah) peeks over the bottom center edge of the card.

Key Phrase:

Financial Troubles

Upright Meaning:

There are serious problems with credit and bills, but it's still possible to get control of your financial worries…perhaps with the help of a specialist? There may be difficulties with lawsuits; if the querent is currently receiving legal or financial advice, it's flawed. It's time to get control of the use of credit, curtail spending habits, and stop living as though consequences will disappear; focus on the future, retirement, and insurance matters.

REVERSED MEANING:

This card reversed implies that the querent is attempting the impossible goal of getting what she/he wants without paying the necessary price. The querent is awash in worry and self-pity as a result of his or her material troubles, yet is resisting all change because of possible failures or "things getting even worse." Deep-seated security issues need to be faced or else the querent will create his or her own self-fulfilled prophecies. Hate underlies his or her actions.

Six of Pentacles

Moon in Taurus (Exaltation) / Tiphereth of Assiah

Description of Illustration:

A brilliant stained-glass window displays a classical Madonna cuddling her newborn Son, with a few variations. In this picture, the Son holds a golden bull. Also, the Moon shines above them with three pentacles on either side, for a total of six, forming an arch above the duo. A golden sphere (Tiphereth) peeks over the bottom center edge of the card.

Key Phrase:

Prosperity

Upright Meaning:

Financial resources are flowing the querent's way; current investments (especially of an artistic nature) will have great value in the future, and any hunches regarding profitable new ventures will flourish. Because the Moon can represent children, this card also reassures the querent that his or her children are stable and will succeed.

Reversed Meaning:

If well aspected, the querent is seeking material comforts and is aware of his or her good fortune. If very poorly aspected, a reversed card can suggest that the querent is overly attached to physical comforts and worrying about unfounded money problems. Conservatism underlies his or her actions.

Seven of Pentacles

Saturn in Taurus / Netzach of Assiah

Description of Illustration:
A large evergreen stands set apart in a snow-covered forest at night. Someone has clearly been decorating the tree for the winter celebrations, as more than half has been decorated with lit candles, fruit, nuts, small wrapped presents, gold coins, and red roses; however, the bottom third of the tree is completely bare. In addition to the other decorations, seven pentacles adorn the tree. At the top of the tree in place of a star we find the planet Saturn, and at the base of the tree the old Holly King stares at his alarmingly empty bag of presents, depressed at his lack of resources to finish his goal of decorating the tree. A lone bull stands in the distance, shaking his great head sorrowfully at the King's plight. A green sphere (Netzach) peeks over the bottom center edge of the card.

Key Phrase:
Discontent

Upright Meaning:
Despite considerable hard work, the querent is in the midst of a difficult period: there are insufficient resources on all levels, from improper nutrition to limited cash. There may be contractual dilemmas, labor disputes, cutbacks, and layoffs. The querent is even befuddled in selecting partnerships.

REVERSED MEANING:
The querent is simply unsatisfied with the results of his or her labors, and bogged down by considerable financial commitment. If poorly aspected, the querent may resort to subterfuge in order to alleviate his or her plight. Despair underlies the querent's actions, and his/her compensation for personal lack of fulfillment is to compulsively STOP others in their endeavors (especially those who are more content) and make them wrong.

Eight of Pentacles

Sun in Virgo / Hod of Assiah

Description of Illustration:
Father Time sits at a table attempting to glue back together a pentacle that has broken into eight pieces, even though one piece is obviously missing. Ironically, seven unbroken pentacles hang on the wall behind him, but he doesn't seem to care. All that matters to him is his inability to fix the broken pentacle! Also behind him is a ticking wall clock in the shape of a Sun. The statue of the Virgin from the Hermit card rests upon Father Time's worktable, but her back is to him. An orange sphere (Hod) peeks over the bottom center edge of the card.

Key Phrase:
Fixation

Upright Meaning:
The current matter is not worth pursuing. It's time for the querent to distance and gain a broader perspective with regards to what's troubling him or her. Whatever the querent has presently invested his or her energy into—whether a diet, a lawyer, or an investment—will not pay off because she/he has missed the big picture.

REVERSED MEANING:

If very well aspected, this card tells the querent that she/he needs to pay more attention to the details. If poorly aspected, she/he is obsessed with aspects of the situation that don't matter while missing the things that do. Often this card reversed suggests that the querent's attention is stuck on a particular viewpoint as a result of the desperate attempt to prove his/her own vision of how things should be, rather than seeing what is. There is a general tone of numbness, as though the querent is fixating on the details to avoid seeing the truth.

Nine of Pentacles

Venus in Virgo (Fall) / Yesod of Assiah

Description of Illustration:

Here we have the divine mysteries of the Shekhinah, Hebrew for the feminine face and aspects of God, in all her glory! A festive holiday wreath hangs upon a front door that is cracked open as the lovely Virgin statue from the Hermit card has come to life, but she is closing the door upon us, preventing us from entering her sweet domain that we can just barely see behind her, which includes a large Yule log with three lit candles rising from it—one white, one red, and one black. The wreath is made of evergreen and is covered with lush apples and pinecones. Nine pentacles are evenly spaced around the wreath, and at the top, in the center of a green velvet bow, is the planet Venus. A purple sphere (Yesod) peeks over the bottom center edge of the card.

Key Phrase:

Inopportunity

Upright Meaning:

Now is not the time for anything new! A situation or person sweetly entices the querent, who is lost in misperception: The timing is wrong and the essentials of the circumstance(s) don't add up. The querent needs to be cautious at work, especially with a woman at work; there will be delays and uncertainty on the part of any partners because they're currently unimpressed with the querent. Wait before making any major decisions or purchases—this is not the time.

REVERSED MEANING:

The querent is entangled in his or her feelings regarding issues of health, love, and work and therefore making ill-timed decisions, more consumed with emotions rather than the facts of the matter. In a man's reading, this card reversed may show an imprudent romantic interest in a woman at work or in a health-related field. If poorly aspected, this card can suggest that the querent is misjudging people at work, being judgmental and selective based upon emotional reactions rather than objectivity. Underlying the querent's emotions is overcompensation for the belief that she/he is fundamentally undeserving.

Ten of Pentacles

MERCURY IN VIRGO (RULER) / MALKUTH OF ASSIAH

DESCRIPTION OF ILLUSTRATION:

A group of magi (Persian experts in astrology, magic, and natural sciences) visit a toddler-age Jesus in his home, offering him gifts of gold, frankincense, and myrrh. By the opulence of the house of Joseph, the father of Jesus, it is clear that he is already a wealthy man. Joseph and Mary hold hands in the background; while Joseph holds the planet Mercury, Mary holds the statue of the Virgin from the Hermit card. Ten perfect pentacles are superimposed upon the picture, forming the image of the Qabalistic Tree of Life. A russet, navy, citrine, and olive sphere (Malkuth) peeks over the bottom center edge of the card.

KEY PHRASE:

Concrete Accomplishment

UPRIGHT MEANING:

This card promises well-deserved job prosperity and wealth. The money that is needed by the querent to pay someone else is coming—either from a settlement or else from another unexpected venue. Because Mercury moves short distances, this card may herald a homecoming or moving to a new and better place. If poorly aspected, this card suggests that the querent needs to plan ahead, as there is an arduous task necessitating patience and attention to detail before taking action; the slow and steady pace

is always preferred when this card comes up. Beware the growing apathy that often accompanies having everything one wants in the material plane.

Reversed Meaning:

If well aspected, the querent is experiencing a state of contented fullness in his or her life; if poorly aspected, she/he may be actively seeking (or worrying about the loss of) wealth and success. A reversed 10 of Pentacles may simply indicate the querent's talents: writing and teaching, a brilliant analytical mind, and a propensity to garner wealth.

The Wands Suit

Ace of Wands

Root of Fire / Kether of Atziluth

Description of Illustration:
The background of this card is filled with flames of fire; in the foreground is a huge hand that holds up a mighty magical wand. Floating above we see a fiery Crown. A white sphere (Kether) peeks over the bottom center edge of the card.

Key Phrase:
Power of Fire

Upright Meaning:
The Fire element is developing in the querent's life right now, bringing desire, creativity, and ample power. Now is the time for potent, forceful action in order to grasp what the querent wants. She/he is strengthened by serenity of beingness.

Reversed Meaning:
If well aspected, the querent possesses the capacity to succeed in the endeavor(s) under consideration; if poorly aspected, the querent believes that she/he will succeed, but there are obstacles that must first be acknowledged and faced. To know the obstacles, look to the surrounding cards.

Two of Wands

Mars in Aries (Ruler) / Chokmah of Atziluth

Description of Illustration:
The Risen King stands triumphant in the Underworld, one leg on a defeated demon of darkness as the rest of the shades and spirits bow before him. He grasps two wands crossing in one hand, and the planet Mars in the other. The ram (from the Emperor card), with the spear still piercing his side, kneels before him. A gray sphere (Chokmah) peeks over the bottom center edge of the card.

Key Phrase:
Aggressive Conquest

Upright Meaning:
It's time to "take the bull by the horns." Lead the others into the new enterprise with gusto! What the situation needs is dominating, aggressive force: If the querent takes control and faces the unknown head-on, then she/he will succeed. Mars can sometimes represent an assertive older woman in the querent's life, depending upon surrounding cards. This card may also forecast a sudden situation or accident coming that will demand impulsive, forceful action on the part of the querent. Exhilaration sustains the querent's efforts.

REVERSED MEANING:

The querent is competitive, needs to be in the lead, and wants to do more, more quickly than anyone else; she/he tends towards belligerence, and mows down others in the overwhelming drive to get his or her own way. Some kind of physical or competitive action is necessary for the well-being of the person asking the question.

Three of Wands

Sun in Aries (Exaltation) / Binah of Atziluth

Description of Illustration:

The Risen King appears to Mary Magdalene for the first time after conquering the Underworld. They hold hands as they gaze into each other's eyes; the Sun is emblazoned on the King's crown and breast as he literally radiates like the Sun. The ram from the 2 of Wands stands regally, happily holding three wands, his side now healed from his previous wound. A black sphere (Binah) peeks over the bottom center edge of the card.

Key Phrase:

Established Strength

Upright Meaning:

The querent's status in the situation is one of assertive, regal, accomplished power with a hint of arrogance. In a woman's reading, this card may suggest a new love encounter with a sincere, younger man. If poorly aspected, there may be a problem with divergent viewpoints within the family, or else a situation that will call for decisive, assertive action on the part of the querent in defense of his or her position. Be careful of monotony.

Reversed Meaning:
This querent is a strong-willed leader, who hates daily tedium and loves initiating new change. If well aspected, the querent has a lucid vision of what needs to be done and how to do it. If poorly aspected, she/he needs to beware of quick action without careful planning, as well as act shrewdly in handling opposing viewpoints that may challenge his or her leadership.

Four of Wands

Venus in Aries (Detriment) / Chesed of Atziluth

Description of Illustration:
A huge multi-colored egg fills this card; however, a large crack splits the egg from top to bottom. Upon closer inspection, it is clear that the egg has been deliberately decorated to hide its imperfections. The planet Venus holds two wands on the left of the card while a ram holds two wands on the right, but they both have their backs to each other in disagreement. A blue sphere (Chesed) peeks over the bottom center edge of the card.

Key Phrase:
Apparent Perfection

Upright Meaning:
The situation(s) has the appearance of perfection, without the substance. Nothing is working in its current form: The querent is at odds with and making poor decisions about his or her lover, any current business deals or partnerships have a feeble foundation, the home is a "house of cards." There are probably even problems with the mother-in-law. Unexpressed resentment obscures everything.

REVERSED MEANING:
    Like the director of his own play, this person is responding to other people as the roles that she/he has assigned to them and critiquing their performance, rather than seeing them for who they actually are. If well aspected, the querent may be a late bloomer in love, is finished with the current relationship, or else has entirely lost the desire to marry. If poorly aspected, the querent is unstable, impetuous, and determined to get what she/he wants…at all costs.

Five of Wands

Saturn in Leo (Detriment) / Geburah of Atziluth

Description of Illustration:
A Catholic priest holds three wands as he angrily fights a Pagan priest who holds two. We can see above them the image of their thoughts and, ironically, they are thinking the same thing as they both picture the Risen King reuniting with his Bride. A lion hangs his head sadly in the background, and the planet Saturn is in the sky above them, directly between them. A red sphere (Geburah) peeks over the bottom center edge of the card.

Key Phrase:
Conflict

Upright Meaning:
This card promises conflict between the parties involved. There will be problems with bosses or authority figures. The querent is generally burned out, run down, and struggling with accumulative, degenerative health problems (such as chronic fatigue syndrome or male impotence) resulting from insecurity issues, blocked vitality, and sexual troubles. There will be impassioned differences between older and younger generations. If very well aspected, this card may bring a much older romantic love interest into the querent's life, but be careful—the dissimilarities may overshadow the desirability of the match.

REVERSED MEANING:
If very well aspected, the querent is intensely concerned and even depressed about the conflict(s) that consume him or her. Otherwise, the querent is bold, rash, insistent that his or her way is right, and unable or unwilling to see the other's point of view. In a man's reading, this card reversed always expresses his basic dissatisfaction with his life, as though in mourning for the lost chances of youth. Hostility lies beneath everything.

Six of Wands

Jupiter in Leo / Tiphereth of Atziluth

Description of Illustration:
The Risen King rides in victory on the backs of a magnificent lion and a humble donkey over palm branches laid beneath their feet; he holds the planet Jupiter in one hand and a mighty wand in the other; five other men holding wands and palm branches bow down before him. A golden sphere (Tiphereth) peeks over the bottom center edge of the card.

Key Phrase:
Victory

Upright Meaning:
Even if poorly aspected, this card promises victory, success, and good luck: no worries. The querent will succeed in overcoming all dilemmas, as well as probably attracting some kind of fame, attention, or leadership opportunity. Everything is buoyed by strong interest.

Reversed Meaning:
The querent is optimistic, loves a good gamble, enjoys children, and takes great pride and satisfaction in his or her own life's circumstances...even if a tad excessively. If very poorly aspected, warn the querent to curtail his or her tendency to gamble and beware of "blowing one's own horn."

Seven of Wands

Mars in Leo / Netzach of Atziluth

Description of Illustration:
Dionysus holds up his fennel and ivy wand in one hand and the pile of Semele's ashes in the other as he confronts Hades, the Lord of the Underworld, upon his dark throne. Hades holds the planet Mars in one hand and a wand in the other, while four fearsome guards on either side of his throne wield their wands like spears; Hades' queen, Persephone, raises her wand in supplication, imploring her stern husband to return Dionysus' mortal mother to him. A proud lion stands next to Dionysus, lending his support. A green sphere (Netzach) peeks over the bottom center edge of the card.

Key Phrase:
Valiant Resistance

Upright Meaning:
At face value, we have a person who has great strength and will to accomplish a goal, but equally strong external forces are working against him/her. There may be trouble with credit or love affairs; this card can even discuss a loss of job or lover because of cross purposes. Attend to a moderate illness or infection resulting from a recent unexpected event, loss, or trauma: It is potentially serious as it affects the basic life force of the body's entire system. Beware of contracting a sexual disease due to reckless seeking of

distraction in pleasant sensations. If very well aspected, this card commends the querent for Herculean effort but still encourages him or her to give up the lost cause and choose a more reasonable course of action.

Reversed Meaning:

If well aspected, the querent is displaying considerable valor in the face of mounting opposition. If not, she/he is behaving as a bully, controlled by his or her impulse for personal gratification, and forcing him or herself into an inappropriate relationship or position. Anxiety makes everything seem even worse than it already is.

Eight of Wands

Mercury in Sagittarius (Detriment) / Hod of Atziluth

Description of Illustration:
At the bottom of the card a weeping Mary Magdalene runs from the open entrance to the Underworld (tomb). Eight wands fly above, quickly passing her. She is unaware of the Centaur (with angel's wings) who approaches her from behind with the good news that the King has returned. The planet Mercury is engraved upon the opening to the Underworld. An orange sphere (Hod) peeks over the bottom center edge of the card.

Key Phrase:
Fleeting Force

Upright Meaning:
The querent is missing the vital details of the current situation because of his or her focus on distant goals and desires. This card advises the querent to slow down because she/he is rushing much too rapidly in all matters. Watch out for speeding tickets, as well as potential problems with paperwork or credentials as a result of not completing the requirements. There may be a temporary visit by a foreigner, a guru, or someone who has been traveling abroad.

REVERSED MEANING:
The querent is acting with an impulsive swiftness that will not endure. She/he may be planning a long trip, investigating a spiritual philosophy, or even considering studying a foreign language: No matter what it is, she/he is rushing into it and will not follow through. Underneath this sudden drive is a desire for propitiation.

Nine of Wands

MOON IN SAGITTARIUS / YESOD OF ATZILUTH

DESCRIPTION OF ILLUSTRATION:
Eostre walks across a verdant green meadow, using her wand as a paintbrush as she paints the flowers and the landscape in vibrant hues. Beside her a white bunny carries glittering rainbow eggs for some children in the distance. Eight wands stand on the horizon behind them; they are in fact eight maypoles; and centaurs, nymphs, and satyrs frolic around them. The full moon rises in the sky above them. A purple sphere (Yesod) peeks over the bottom center edge of the card.

KEY PHRASE:
Boundless Potential

UPRIGHT MEANING:
Boundless potential exists for the querent to accomplish his or her goals. A long journey, going overseas, or a major move is in the future. Now is the perfect time to pursue a college degree or follow a spiritual aspiration. Because the Moon often signifies a child, this card can show that the querent's children will attain their goals. This card brings a cause for optimism no matter how negative the surrounding cards.

REVERSED MEANING:

If well aspected, this card describes the querent as an imaginative optimist who believes that honesty and ideals are more important than any relationship. If very poorly aspected, it suggests that the querent tends to be dogmatic about his or her extreme and unorthodox ideas. An unspoken goal of making amends is behind the far-reaching aims of the querent.

Ten of Wands

Saturn in Sagittarius / Malkuth of Atziluth

Description of Illustration:

The huge feet of seven dead Titans, burned by Zeus' lightning bolt wand, lie in a semi-circle around a black cauldron with the planet Saturn emblazoned upon it; Dionysus, in the form of a bull, has been torn apart into seven pieces—each one skewered on one of the Titan's mighty wands. Six of the pieces have been eaten and charred, but one piece—the heart—remains whole. A sad Centaur picks up Dionysus' own beautiful boyish head in mourning. Dionysus' own wand lies discarded on the floor, yet from his blood grows a lovely pomegranate tree, forming a stronger, new wand. A russet, navy, citrine, and olive sphere (Malkuth) peeks over the bottom center edge of the card.

Key Phrase:

Oppression

Upright Meaning:

Beware! This is a time of stress, oppression, and suppression from unexpected sources. There may be a challenging encounter with suppressive philosophies coming, or else a confrontation with an older person who fiercely objects to the querent's current purposes. The querent is assuming responsibility for situations that are out of his/her reach.

REVERSED MEANING:
The querent is overwhelmed, going in too many directions at once, and could suffer a nervous breakdown from sheer overloading of him or herself. Hopelessness confuses the situation.

The Cups Suit

Ace of Cups

Root of Water / Kether of Briah

Description of Illustration:
A huge hand reaches out from the clouds and proffers a golden chalice filled with blood and water. In the background is the powerful ocean. Floating above we see a watery Crown. A white sphere (Kether) peeks over the bottom center edge of the card.

Key Phrase:
Power of Water

Upright Meaning:
Within the querent, the Water element is churning and broiling, broadening the querent's intuition and emotions. A new relationship (possibly, but not necessarily, romantic) is on the horizon. Perhaps the querent is artistic. Now is the time to embark upon a spiritual quest. If poorly aspected and the querent has asked about a partner, this card suggests that the other is a lazy, pleasure-seeking opportunist (all the worst aspects of the water element). Use postulates to expand the possibilities.

Reversed Meaning:
The querent will either be seeking a new relationship or else focusing his or her energies upon plumbing the emotional depths within. If well aspected, the querent would do well to follow his or her instincts right now. If poorly aspected, the querent could be caught up in the quagmire of his or her raging emotions, or else dissipated and full of pretense (the worst aspects of the water element).

Two of Cups

Venus in Cancer / Chokmah of Briah

Description of Illustration:
A radiant bride and nervous groom exchange their vows together on the beach as the planet Venus arises from the sea foam to preside over their union. The bride and groom each clasp large golden chalices, and the groom has tipped his chalice towards his love's, pouring some of his elixir into hers. Watching the ceremony we see none other than the Green Man, Gaia, Sir Galahad, and puck. A large crab (symbolizing Cancer) sits on the beach to the right of the couple, enjoying the wedding, and an intricate sand castle has been built to their left. A gray sphere (Chokmah) peeks over the bottom center edge of the card.

Key Phrase:
True Love

Upright Meaning:
In matters of love, this is the real thing. There will be harmonious love and family relationships, possibly a family inheritance or reunion. This card may predict an addition to the family, either by marriage or birth. Enthusiasm uplifts everything.

Reversed Meaning:
The querent is either searching for love or else wonders if she/he has found it. The querent may desire reconciliation with his or her spouse, mother, or family.

Three of Cups

Mercury in Cancer / Binah of Briah

Description of Illustration:
The hobgoblin Puck, surrounded by three tempting female faeries that are especially different and equally appealing, is unable to choose between them. The setting is a sandy beach; a tiny crab is at Puck's heels, about to grasp him with its pincers. Each of the three faeries holds a golden cup in one hand, and it is clear that Puck is quite thirsty! Each faerie also clasps an object behind her back, hiding it from Puck; the faerie on the left holds a rock, the faerie on the right holds a twig, and the faerie closest to us holds the planet Mercury. A black sphere (Binah) peeks over the bottom center edge of the card.

Key Phrase:
Abundance

Upright Meaning:
If well aspected, the querent is experiencing a period of abundance and operating from an attitude of "the more the merrier" right now; she/he is probably either finding pleasure in multiple relationships rather than in commitment to one person, or else is surrounded by multiple romantic opportunities. If poorly aspected, this card suggests that the querent (or someone in the querent's life) is having an affair.

Reversed Meaning:

The querent is either being tempted to cheat on his or her significant other or else suspects another of cheating. Conversely, she/he may be consumed with an all-pervasive desire for more. If very well aspected, this card can indicate remarkable ingenuity in the realms of speaking and writing on the part of the querent. Boredom feeds the drive for excess.

Four of Cups

Moon in Cancer (Ruler) / Chesed of Briah

Description of Illustration:
Gaia holds two golden chalices, one in each hand, and balances a third one upon the ocean of her belly; on the first cup is engraved a crescent moon, on the second cup is a half moon, and the cup upon her belly is engraved with a full moon. The Sky, her husband, with his hands made of clouds, offers her a fourth chalice engraved with the image of the crab, but she seems unwilling to take it from him. A blue sphere (Chesed) peeks over the bottom center edge of the card.

Key Phrase:
Blended Pleasure

Upright Meaning:
It is a time of blended pleasure for the querent; she/he will remain in the present situation, yet won't be completely satisfied. If poorly aspected, there may be troubles with hormones, menstruation, menopause, or children. Because of the basic dominance of the feminine inherent in this card, in a man's reading it may show bisexuality, effeminacy, a lack of sexual balance, or a strong attachment to the mother. Things tend to last at least four years (seeming far too long to the querent) in Cancer.

REVERSED MEANING:
If well aspected, the querent demonstrates a high level of emotional maturity, nurturing, self-sacrifice, and awareness of the needs and feelings of others, especially with regards to his or her children; if poorly aspected, this card can show that the querent is suffering from too much feminine influence and is overly sensitive to the reactions of others. There is an unwillingness to leave home or make any change that might adversely affect another. Resentment underlies his or her lack of action.

Five of Cups

Mars in Scorpio (Classical Ruler) / Geburah of Briah

Description of Illustration:
It is Sunset at the ocean, and the sky is a mixture of darkening hues. Sir Percival faces us as he leads his weary horse, both their heads bowed in exhaustion. He stares at four golden chalices that lie on the ground before him, knocked over and spilling what could be either wine or blood upon the sand. Shining in the sky behind him we see Sir Galahad, clasping the Holy Grail as he steps into the City of the Spirit amongst the clouds. A scorpion plays amongst the fallen chalices, and the planet Mars rises above the horizon. A red sphere (Geburah) peeks over the bottom center edge of the card.

Key Phrase:
Heartbreak

Upright Meaning:
This card portends sadness, depression, bankruptcy, financial disaster, personal failures, and emotional distress in an ever-increasing downward spiral. Even if well aspected, the querent is currently or will soon experience a profound loss in pleasure. This calls for severe, controlled action in order to cope with these mounting tribulations.

REVERSED MEANING:

If very well aspected, this card reveals the querent's inner strength to transform or change a seemingly impossible situation. Normally, however, this card reversed reveals the querent to be internally awash in anger, depression, pain, and loss. It often suggests that she/he may be over-reacting to a perceived hurt, rather than a real one. The querent must find a healthy release to his or her pain by recognizing its true source. Pain is not the problem, it is the avoidance of pain and blaming others and outside circumstances that is the problem. The message of this card is to cease avoiding the discomfort of pain, and instead seek its cause, for it is only in facing the cause of our pain that we can discover its cure.

Six of Cups

Sun in Scorpio / Tiphereth of Briah

Description of Illustration:

The Green Man dances with wild abandon on the beach around a Midsummer Night's bonfire; he holds a golden chalice engraved with the Sun in his left hand and a chalice engraved with a scorpion in his right hand. On one side of the Green Man a nymph and a satyr are on the beach in the throes of lovemaking, two standing chalices besides them. On the opposite side of the Green Man a satyr abandons his unsatisfied nymph, kicking their cups aside as he leaves, quitting their lovemaking before they have even begun. A golden sphere (Tiphereth) peeks over the bottom center edge of the card.

Key Phrase:

Sensuality

Upright Meaning:

This is an exaggerated time of sensual excess for the querent—with lots of changes and high moments immediately followed by low ones. There may also be extreme changes in handling other people's money, especially in the realms of debt and taxes, often of a legal nature. This card warns the querent not to prematurely quit: Finish what has been started. Often heralds a drastic life-change.

REVERSED MEANING:
Instead of facing his/her pain, the querent is seeking pleasure in sensation to compensate. The querent exhibits an extreme black and white mentality and has trouble setting healthy boundaries or accepting the boundaries set by others. If poorly aspected, there may be extremes in sexual behavior, control issues, and power struggles. If well aspected, the querent may be single-mindedly curious about the deeper mysteries of life and seeking self-improvement. The truth of mild interest is being overcompensated for with excessive passion.

Seven of Cups

VENUS IN SCORPIO (DETRIMENT) / NETZACH OF BRIAH

DESCRIPTION OF ILLUSTRATION:
This card depicts a family that is vacationing on the beach together, but they are in the midst of a HUGE family fight. The father and mother are lying on lounge chairs, sunburned and red-faced from shouting at each other, but even as the father yells, his eyes can't help watching the shapely blond in the pink bikini walk by. The older brother and sister sit in stony silence; their arms are folded and their backs are to each other. The youngest boy is holding his foot and crying next to an unfinished sand castle he's been building; a small scorpion (who is being ridden by a mischievous Puck) has just stung him, but everyone else is so involved in the fight that they haven't yet noticed. The unfinished sand castle has seven turrets that look like seven golden cups—each one filled with a different unreachable dream desired by the little boy. The first holds a dragon, the second holds a little girl, the third contains Gaia, the fourth has toys, the fifth is full of riches, the sixth holds Sir Galahad, and the seventh holds a happy, loving home. A beach ball that looks suspiciously like the planet Venus sits next to the little boy, unnoticed. The Green Man's face sadly peers at the scene from amongst the foliage of a nearby palm tree. A green sphere (Netzach) peeks over the bottom center edge of the card.

KEY PHRASE:
Poisonous Illusions

Upright Meaning:

This card portends losing oneself in illusion to escape internal emptiness, for as the sensations and interactions of the physical universe cease to satisfy the individual, she/he begins attributing significance to the dream of satisfaction itself, thereby attempting to artificially craft the emptiness of experience to mean something more. There will be extreme energy imbalances; a poison is invading the querent's life. This card may caution the querent of a serious infection to be attended to immediately, or else counsel against the overspending of money for frivolity and comfort (perhaps even using another person's credit). There may be heated fights and secrets kept between partners. Watch out for a purely sexual affair of the "fatal attraction" variety. This card may warn of an abusive or suppressive person in the querent's life. If very well aspected, this card could indicate an inheritance from a female relative or else financial gain because of someone else's money, probably through a marriage or partnership.

Reversed Meaning:

Often this card in the reversed position indicates that the querent is keeping a deep secret that is literally poisoning him or her internally. Poorly aspected, this card may suggest that the querent is abusive or suppressive. In a man's reading, it can reveal a negative connection with his mother which has "poisoned" his relationships with women ever since. The querent may be hiding a secret love affair, secretly jealous of another, or else lost in the illusion of beauty and the ideal woman in a hopeless attempt to escape hungering emptiness. This card may also indicate extreme confusion and trauma regarding sexuality, to which the querent has responded with extremes: she/he could be a nymphomaniac or else a forty-five year old virgin. Terror underlies the compulsive need to keep everything hidden.

Eight of Cups

Saturn in Pisces / Hod of Briah

Description of Illustration:

It is harvest time, and the fields of wheat are burgeoning (like the pregnant belly of Gaia) under the scorching heat as the farmers toil in the fields. Eight farmers rest as they wipe their sweaty brows and drink from their eight golden cups. One farmer, however, is fed up with the back-breaking work, and he is abandoning the fields; his back is to us as he wears a traveling cloak with the image of the planet Saturn embroidered upon it, walking stick in hand, as he follows a stream towards the ocean far in the distance, where we can just make out the two fish of Pisces playing joyfully. Two of the farmers at rest make fun of their departing co-worker. An orange sphere (Hod) peeks over the bottom center edge of the card.

Key Phrase:

Abandoned Success

Upright Meaning:

This is a situation of abandoned success: If the querent will only persevere, things will work out. Lethargy and lassitude are the paths of least resistance, but don't be fooled. She/he is missing or giving up too soon on an important opportunity. There may be hidden trouble at work, as well as things going on behind the querent's back. This card assures the querent that she/he is not too old to succeed.

REVERSED MEANING:

The querent feels as though she/he has lost what's important and is "over the hill," wanting to give up and not seeing beyond the present apparent hopelessness of the situation. Perhaps she/he is over-empathizing with someone else's loss, finding it difficult to refrain from helping and therefore losing self-identity in the instinct to not "abandon" another. If well aspected, this card reversed may indicate that the querent is beginning to separate from the external world and focus inwards. Grief often underlies these longings.

Nine of Cups

Jupiter in Pisces (Classical Ruler) / Yesod of Briah

Description of Illustration:

Puck lolls, contentedly inebriated, in a large, golden chalice engraved with two fishes swimming counter-clockwise around the planet Jupiter; the large chalice lies in the center of a circle of eight smaller chalices which are overflowing with ephemeral delights—wine, money, drugs, gambling, rich foods, shopping excursions, love-making, and even religious fervor. In vain, Puck is trying to hide a huge bottle of alcohol behind his back, as though to convince both the viewer and himself that he hasn't had a sip. A purple sphere (Yesod) peeks over the bottom center edge of the card.

Key Phrase:

Indulgence

Upright Meaning:

If well aspected, gladness and festivity. Generally, intoxicating immersion in material happiness to the point of gluttony. If poorly aspected, there may be hidden alcoholism, drug problems, codependency, or seduction. Be wary of superfluous spending, gratuitous sex, getting fat, and the negative affects of too much celebration. If very poorly aspected, everything may not be as wonderful as it seems—watch out for ulterior motives.

REVERSED MEANING:
    If well aspected, the querent is seeking happiness and bliss—either through celebration and indulgence or else through religion and seclusion. If poorly aspected, she/he is easily deceived and exploited. There is a level of distraction as the querent throws him—or herself—into enjoyable experiences to avoid confrontation of self.

Ten of Cups

Mars in Pisces / Malkuth of Briah

Description of Illustration:
On a tree-covered cliff in front of the ocean, the jovial Green Man sits atop of an oak tree controlling a marionette puppet—a smaller version of himself that stands on the ground beneath the tree. The puppet Green man has no idea that he is being controlled. Across from the puppet master, Green Man floats the planet Mars, also controlling a marionette, the young Sir Galahad. Sir Galahad is equally unaware of his strings as he happily grasps the largest cup in a rainbow arch of 10 cups that float in the sky between the two puppet masters. The puppet master Green Man looks out of the corner of this narrowed eyes at the planet Mars as the puppet Green Man, seeing the strings on his companion, reaches towards Galahad's strings with a large knife, attempting to free Galahad in such a way that Galahad doesn't notice that he's being freed. On the surface, it appears that the puppet Green man is attempting to free his friend from the confines of the strings; however, the real question is: Will an individual so unaware of his own condition truly be able to help another, or will his "help" only cause further pain and suffering? (What happens to a puppet with no stings?) And even more insidious to consider, is the desire to "help" the puppet's own, or simply the cover up for the mysterious intentions of the puppet master by whom he is

controlled? Two distant fish in the ocean watch with interest. A russet, navy, citrine, and olive sphere (Malkuth) peeks over the bottom center edge of the card.

KEY PHRASE:
Happiness

UPRIGHT MEANING:
Attainment of emotional ideals, often to the detriment of the individual. The querent will soon (or already has) successfully arranged his/her emotive and relational life to be truly happy, but hidden underneath this satisfaction lays the warning of incapacitating complacency. The 10 of Cups cautions us that when we are too focused on happiness, we lose the will to change; it lulls us into contented inaction and acceptance of the status quo, shielding our eyes from the facts of the evils and injustices of this world, for it is discomfort and distress that motivate us to improve and grow. The panacea of our modern age is the lie of the pursuit of happiness as an end unto itself. This card may also warn the querent to beware of an aggressive, hidden enemy or some sort of spiritual manipulation: Someone is not being up front with the querent or else is taking advantage of him or her. The querent's ideals have created a risky relationship or situation from which it will be difficult to breakout. If very well aspected, the querent may be called to an important spiritual quest, but doesn't see it yet.

REVERSED MEANING:
When well aspected, this card suggests that the querent is a devoted, imaginative idealist who doesn't see the darker sides of existence. Otherwise, the querent may want to escape the situation that she/he has created, for she/he is blinded by ideals to the reality of the situation. Perhaps the querent is dedicated to the pursuit of happiness to the exclusion of all else. If poorly aspected, the querent is untrustworthy, has a hidden agenda, and enforces his or her rigid view of "what is" on everyone. Heady idealism conceals a feeling of uselessness.

The Swords Suit

Ace of Swords

Root of Air / Kether of Yetzirah

Description of Illustration:
A huge hand holds up a formidable sword that pierces through an airy crown. Behind the sword is the wind swept sky filled with a mighty storm as two powerful winds battle and stir up the leaves of autumn. A white sphere (Kether) peeks over the bottom center edge of the card.

Key Phrase:
Power of Air

Upright Meaning:
The Ace of Swords can often herald a new message, contact, or discussion. This card usually portends a powerful beginning in the realm of Air, involving intellect, conflict, or communication. Sometimes this card announces a new relationship (because of its association with Libra). Generally, this card promises the querent a powerful position with regards to these matters. She/he is strengthened by an objective games condition.

Reversed Meaning:
If well aspected, the querent possesses the capacity to succeed in the endeavor(s) under consideration; if poorly aspected, the querent may be seeking a conflict or communication, but there are obstacles that must first be acknowledged and faced.

To know the obstacles, look to the surrounding cards. If very poorly aspected, the querent may be trying to prove that she/he is right or justify his/her actions rather than confront the facts.

Two of Swords

Moon in Libra / Chokmah of Yetzirah

Description of Illustration:
In the foreground, the Lord of Misrule holds two swords crossed across his breast—he is blindfolded, but one eye is peeking through as he smiles mischievously. In the background, two men are shaking hands in front of a medieval castle, closing a deal. The Moon shines above, as one man holds Libra's balanced scales. A gray sphere (Chokmah) peeks over the bottom center edge of the card.

Key Phrase:
Harmony

Upright Meaning:
Peace will be restored, but the truce will not be permanent because the issues are not truly resolved. The querent will handle his or her opponents effectively and his or her relational problems will improve. There will be a positive settlement of any legal disputes. If well aspected and the querent does not have a partner, then a new partnership may be coming. If she/he does have a current partner, this card suggests that the relationship will reach a new level of contractual commitment.

REVERSED MEANING:
The querent is seeking harmony, regardless of the costs to self or others. If well aspected, the querent has the common sense necessary to successfully handle his or her opponents. This card may also suggest that the querent wants to get married. Cheerfulness underlies the querent's objective for amity.

Three of Swords

SATURN IN LIBRA (EXALTATION) / BINAH OF YETZIRAH

DESCRIPTION OF ILLUSTRATION:
Hecate sobs against an autumn landscape as she holds a large red heart that has been torn in two—three swords pierce the heart, and the one that runs from top to bottom seems to hold the heart together. A great veiled chasm is behind Hecate, separating her from her Beloved King in the Underworld. The planet Saturn is in the sky, and the King holds Libra's balanced scales. A black sphere (Binah) peeks over the bottom center edge of the card.

KEY PHRASE:
Separations

UPRIGHT MEANING:
Loss and separations. Sorrow resulting from the loss of a partnership, a job, or a court case. This card may signify a lost item or circumstance that will never be regained. This card can also herald the separation or ending of a relationship, either through break up, divorce, or even physical death. The arrangements of prior agreements or partnerships need to be renegotiated: Their structure has altered to such a degree that they are obsolete, so it is time to either let go of them or else create a new foundation. If poorly aspected, this card may warn of serious illness. If well aspected, these losses will ultimately benefit the querent; conversely, the positive influence

of Saturn may suggest that the querent will marry late in life, or else choose a significantly older, career-oriented spouse.

REVERSED MEANING:

Generally, this card reversed suggests that the querent is either afraid that his or her current partnership is ending, or else wants out of it badly. If well aspected, this desire is justified. If poorly aspected, the querent's reasons for leaving (or not leaving) are inadequate—she/he may be promising more to a partner than can possibly be given, or else unable to make the painful but necessary decisions about the current partnership. Sometimes, if very well aspected, this card suggests that the querent is willing to work hard and determined to make a flawed partnership last. Antagonism is complicating the problems.

Four of Swords

Jupiter in Libra / Chesed of Yetzirah

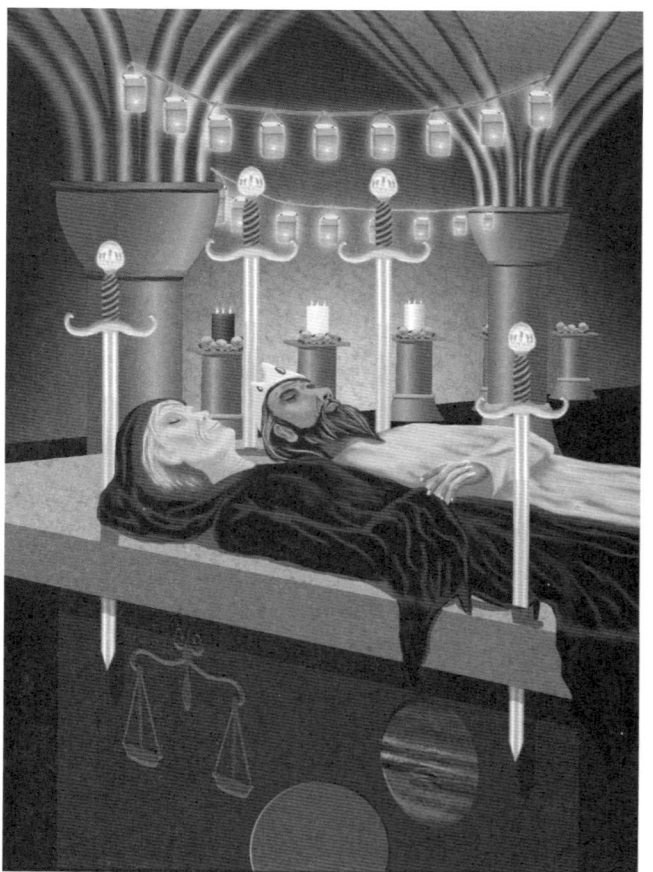

Description of Illustration:

Hecate is with her Beloved King, their hands joined with faces relaxed in eternal peace, as both lie upon a raised dais in an underground royal crypt. We are not sure if they are dead, or simply asleep. Four swords surround them, stuck into the dais like four swords in the stone. The planet Jupiter and Libra's balanced scales are engraved upon the stone dais. Yellow marigolds and luminaries have been used to lovingly adorn the crypt. A blue sphere (Chesed) peeks over the bottom center edge of the card.

Key Phrase:
Partnership

Upright Meaning:

The querent will expand his or her life through interactions with others; she/he is entering a period of rest from stress in which the current problems will be solved. There may be a like-minded, spiritually progressive "soul mate" relationship entering the querent's life. Any professional consulted for assistance (from lawyer to marriage counselor) will bring success. The querent will succeed in helping conflicting parties to resolve their differences as well as in negotiating a business deal to the benefit of all involved. If poorly aspected, this card calls for the querent to meditate and contemplate on the issue before making a decision: There may be a tendency to jump into grand speculations without thoroughly weighing all sides.

REVERSED MEANING:

If poorly aspected, the querent may be trying to satisfy all involved, and therefore satisfying none. Perhaps she/he is looking for his or her "soul mate" or desires a new business partnership. If well aspected, the querent knows that she/he is blessed in his or her partnership(s) and is benefiting financially, emotionally, and spiritually. The querent may be a powerful negotiator and diplomat, or even a professional judge or lawyer. There is a lack of sympathy that strengthens the ability to be objective.

Five of Swords

VENUS IN AQUARIUS / GEBURAH OF YETZIRAH

DESCRIPTION OF ILLUSTRATION:

There is a chaotic line made of five swords strewn across the center of the card. Underneath the swords, a sad Persephone is trapped in the Underworld clasping the planet Venus to her breast like a magical crystal ball—Persephone longs for her mother, Ceres (Roman name, Demeter), the goddess of the harvest. Above the line, Ceres wanders the Earth, mourning her lost daughter. The landscape is dying (summer turning to fall) around her, mirroring her grief. In the background, a cascading waterfall is formed by the mermaid from the Star card, the water-bearer, pouring both her pitchers towards the earth in woe. A red sphere (Geburah) peeks over the bottom center edge of the card.

KEY PHRASE:

Longing

UPRIGHT MEANING:

The querent is caught in circumstances that were originally beautiful, but have now turned ugly; the dreams and ideals of the querent's that should have been sweet have turned into nightmares—relationship(s) have gone sour, there has been betrayal, there is poor public opinion, and activities that at first seemed important are now a complete waste of time. Watch out for health problems from eating too many sweets, like diabetes. Venus may bring love into the querent's life, but ultimately it won't work. If the

querent is currently in a relationship, they are living separate lives. If very well aspected, a current friendship may develop into romance, or else the querent may actually benefit from another's losses.

Reversed Meaning:

The querent feels defeated and hopeless because of his or her failure to accomplish his or her dreams. She/he is probably mourning or refusing to let go of a lost love. If currently involved with someone, the querent is emotionally distancing from the partner. Sometimes this card suggests that the querent may be seeking an open relationship or else has a romantic interest in a friend. If very well aspected, this card can suggest that the querent doesn't think that his or her lover is "the One"—but she/he is mistaken, for this is the Real Thing. Often people with this card reversed are projecting their own romantic notions and past history with women (especially their mothers) upon the other, failing to see their partner as she/he truly is. If poorly aspected and in a woman's reading, she may be an old, lonely spinster who needs to get out into the world more. There is unexpressed anger at the root of the querent's grief.

Six of Swords

Mercury in Aquarius (Exaltation) / Tiphereth of Yetzirah

Description of Illustration:
According to the traditions of the Mexican culture, October 31st is the only day that Death doesn't work. On this card, we have the Lord of Death, Mictlantecutli, taking a vacation as a great owl ferries him across the immense river that is a spirit's first obstacle to enter the underworld. Six swords stand up from the boat, each one pierced through jack-o'-lanterns, sculls, cempasuchil (yellow marigolds—the flower of death in Mexico), and the planet Mercury. The ghost of the mermaid from the Star card (the water-bearer) can be seen in the distance, the water from her two ghostly pitchers defying gravity as they pour upwards. A golden sphere (Tiphereth) peeks over the bottom center edge of the card.

Key Phrase:
Fresh Horizons

Upright Meaning:
There's good news coming! This card encourages the querent that she/he is leaving an inferior situation for a superior one. There will be well-earned successes as well as good advice from friends. The querent will soon realize his or her dreams of travel, education, and philanthropy. Even if poorly aspected, the querent will ultimately benefit from a radical change.

REVERSED MEANING:
   The querent is actively seeking an innovative solution to the current situation. She/he is intelligent, impartial, honest, open, and may be a teacher or humanitarian. Even if poorly aspected, this card portrays the querent in a positive light. She/he is ultimately contented.

Seven of Swords

MOON IN AQUARIUS / NETZACH OF YETZIRAH

DESCRIPTION:
   Persephone sits at Hades' table in the Underworld. The table is resplendently decorated for a Samhein celebration, and the shades of dead people serve their food. Hades gloats as the unknowing Persephone takes a bite of the pomegranate, therefore sealing her fate to be his wife in the Underworld for six months out of every year. Persephone's chair is made of seven swords, and her crown is made of crescent moons; the centerpiece of the table is the ghost of the mermaid from the Star card (the water-bearer), only this time salty tears drip from her two pitchers onto the table. A green sphere (Netzach) peeks over the bottom center edge of the card.

KEY PHRASE:
   Futility

UPRIGHT MEANING:
   Unstable effort arising from impossible dreams and good intentions. There may be broken promises, lies, or misinformation of the public. Watch for thievery; the querent may lose his or her resources by trusting the wrong person(s). Avoid joining losing causes. If there is suspicion of betrayal or deceit, the querent is correct—the person can't be trusted. If the querent is expecting

financial resources of some sort, she/he had better check up on it, because it is not what was promised.

Reversed Meaning:

If well aspected, the querent is a hopeless idealist who is easily fooled. Generally, the querent over-thinks and rationalizes everything and is deceiving him or herself. If poorly aspected, the querent is a liar and is possibly lying to the reader. In addition, Moon in Aquarius is the classical combination to denote an Astrologer. Fear of ultimate failure lies underneath the querent's futile devotion.

Eight of Swords

Jupiter in Gemini (Detriment) / Hod of Yetzirah

Description of Illustration:
The Lord of Misrule dances at a Medieval banquet, only at this feast everything seems to be topsy-turvy in some way. All of the artwork and decorations are upside down and askew, and everyone wears masks. The king bows to a beggar that sits upon his thrown as he hands him a makeshift crown emblazoned with the planet Jupiter; the queen stands on the banquet table, bound, blindfolded, and laughing, as the Lord of Misrule places a circle of eight swords around her. The boy and the girl from the Lovers card sit at the banquet table. An orange sphere (Hod) peeks over the bottom center edge of the card.

Key Phrase:
Shortsighted

Upright Meaning:
The querent is not seeing the situation(s) clearly right now. There will be unfounded speculation, misapplied ideas, and snap decisions based upon little substance. This card can even suggest that the querent needs new glasses or a new hearing aid to help him or her perceive things more accurately. On the positive side, the querent might be a gifted actor, beautician, or some other profession adept at image and appearance. There may be a spiritual or

religious teacher in the querent's life who is much more concerned with how things look, rather than what things actually are.

Reversed Meaning:

The querent is blind to the truth but is excellent at bluffing his or her way through life, having quick wits with little substance; it is important to the querent that others are impressed by his or her "knowledge." This card reversed may also suggest that the querent's focus upon image and appearance, such as fashion, movies, or beauty; if poorly aspected, the querent may be claiming a guru status that she/he doesn't deserve. Sympathy is blinding the querent to the truth of the matter.

Nine of Swords

Mars in Gemini / Yesod of Yetzirah

Description of Illustration:

We are looking at two neighboring houses at night on October 31st. One house is decorated for Samhein, the other for Halloween. The Halloween house has the planet Mars etched upon its door, while the Samhein house has the boy and girl from the Lovers card peeking out its window. The goddess Hecate stands at the crossroads as a fence made of nine swords divides the two houses, and the woman of each house stands on her side of the fence, arguing with the other. A purple sphere (Yesod) peeks over the bottom center edge of the card.

Key Phrase:
Cruelty

Upright Meaning:

The 9 of Swords admonishes that when we believe ourselves to be victims of cruelty, we use this to justify our own cruel victimization of others. When our life seems a nightmare, we drag the nightmare around with us to disturb the lives of those around us. Watch out for suffering as a result of arguments—in the neighborhood, with brothers and sisters, or with an older woman. There will be loud noises and jarring energy surrounding the querent, resulting in troubled dreams and lack of rest or sleep. It is time to take decisive action to put an end to the discord, for neither party will ever see eye to eye as long as each is stuck in his or her own viewpoint. There may be a lack of proper credentials or paperwork, as well as possible fights over contracts. The querent may be heatedly questioned by a hostile source. Beware malicious gossip or any news stories about oneself right now.

Reversed Meaning:

Generally, this card reveals the querent to be actively involved in heated arguments based upon a dogmatic viewpoint. If poorly aspected, the querent is being deliberately malicious and cruel in the process of attempting to win. If well aspected, this card reversed indicates that the querent is concerned about the dissension surrounding him or her right now and wants it to end; she/he wants to get to the bottom of the matter, cutting through the appearances. This card can also signify an investigative reporter who cuts through the mystery to build a breaking news story. The querent justifies his or her behavior by the belief that she/he is a victim.

Ten of Swords

Sun in Gemini / Malkuth of Yetzirah

Description of Illustration:
During an autumn Sunset, we are outside at a somber funeral in a cemetery. The dead man in the casket is lying on his stomach, with nine swords sticking out of his bloody back. Mictlantecutli is amongst the melancholy mourners, disguised to look exactly like the rest of them, only he has a smirk on his face as he holds the tenth sword, still covered with the dead man's blood. No one seems to notice the Lord of Death as he whispers something malicious to the boy and girl from the Lovers card. A red Sun shines on the crimson horizon. A russet, navy, citrine, and olive sphere (Malkuth) peeks over the bottom center edge of the card.

Key Phrase:
Ruin

Upright Meaning:
The damage in the current situation(s) is already done. Words will (or have) cause ruin in some way; the querent should watch his or her reputation, for people are gossiping and backstabbing. If very well aspected, there may be a critical upcoming communication with brothers or sisters, many short trips, an important conversation, or some sort of image-based contact—possibly with the media.

REVERSED MEANING:

Normally, this card reversed suggests that the querent is struggling with feelings of failure and ruin. If poorly aspected, the querent is intellectually arrogant, image-driven, two-faced, superficial, and damages others with his or her thoughtless words. This may be a message to the querent to avoid gossiping, for his or her own cruel words will bring ruin. The querent may be seeking to move on to the next new and exciting experience rather than face the failure of the current situation. Underlying the fear of failure is the ultimate fear of dying.

Notes

Notes

Chapter Four

Tarot Spreads

The Triangle Spread

The triangle is a shape that creates balance and symmetry between three apparently opposing points, just like the three triangles on the Tree of Life. Shuffle, cut, and fan the cards as you focus upon a particular situation in your life (or the querent's) in which you need guidance. Choose three cards, laying the first card to the left, the second card to the right, and the last card in the center beneath the first two, forming an inverted triangle.

CARD ONE:
The Problem

CARD TWO:
The Way Through the Problem

CARD THREE:
The Outcome

Card One reveals the truth that needs to be faced in the current situation.
Card Two shows what must be done in order to face and conquer the challenges presented by the first card.
Card Three predicts what will happen in the situation if the recommendation of the second card is followed.

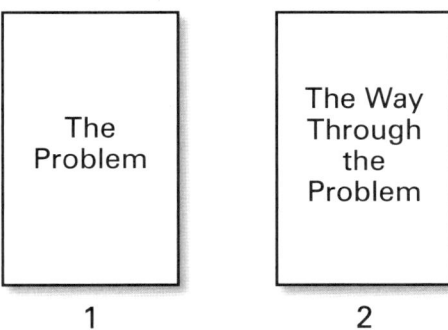

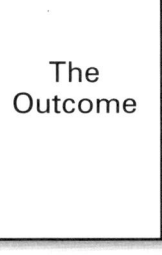

The Cross Spread

The cross is an ancient symbol, much older than the Christian tradition with which it is most commonly associated today, and can be found in numerous sacred traditions throughout antiquity. At its most basic level, it is a symbol of the two intersecting paths that spirits travel upon throughout existence—the vertical axis is one of progression, where each is either on an upward journey towards spirit or a downward journey towards matter; the horizontal axis represents our actions inside the realm of time, justice, cause, and effect. The Celts overlaid the basic cross with an additional sacred symbol, the circle of the Sun, representing the circle of life, the cycle of the seasons, and at each place that an axis intersects the circle, we have the cardinal directions—north, south, east and west—as well as the elements—earth, air, fire, and water, with spirit residing at the center. The Cross Spread is thus named because its shape looks like an equilateral cross.

After thoroughly shuffling the deck, cut the deck three times—once for each Triad on the Tree of Life—and from the top of the deck, lay out ten cards in the form of a Cross.

The Significator:
In a general reading about a person, this represents the querent; with regards to a specific question, this represents the situation.
(This is the Ascendant of the reading.)

Crossing Card:
Reveals what is currently "crossing" (blocking, impeding) the querent or the situation.
(This is like the South Node of the Moon.)

What's Beneath:
What information does the querent already know that forms the foundation of the question?

What's Above:
What information is obvious, but the querent currently is not seeing it?

What's Passing:
What has occurred recently in the querent's life; what is passing away from the querent's life?

The Immediate Future:
What is in store for the querent in the immediate future? (This is the Descendant of the reading.)

Internal World:
What is the internal world of the querent? What is she/he bringing to the situation?

External World:
What is the external world of the querent? What is surrounding him or her?

Distant Past:
What past issue or problem is the querent still carrying in the present that is blurring his or her ability to clearly perceive the situation today?

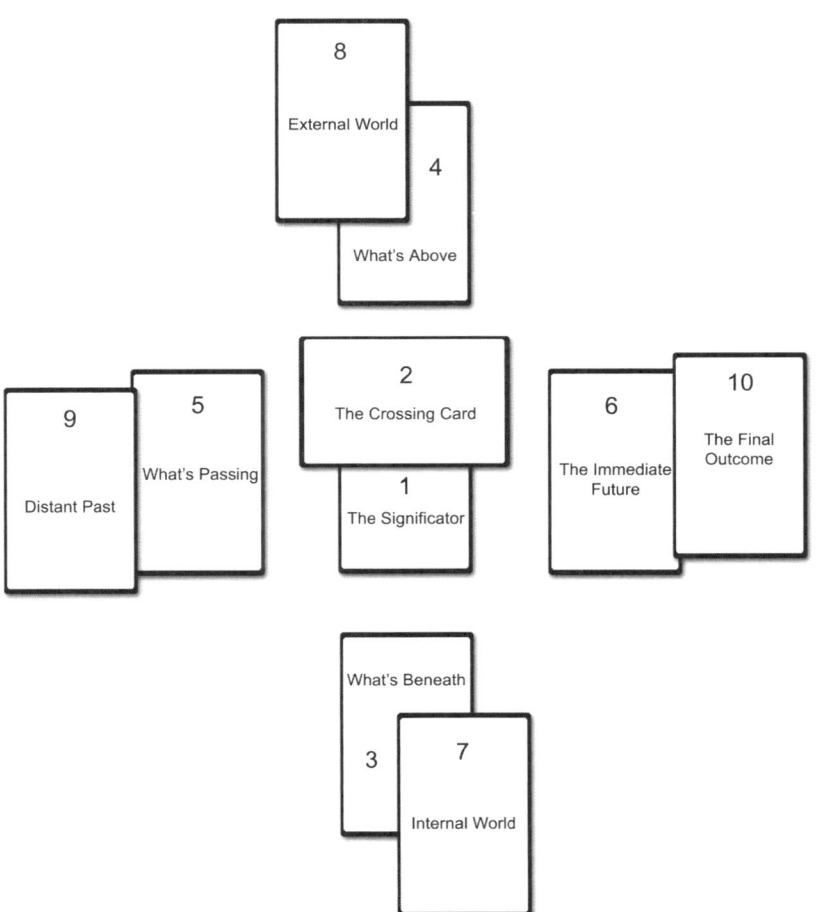

THE FINAL OUTCOME:

What is the ultimate outcome of this situation? What is the main message that the querent must understand in order to grow?

(This is like the North Node of the Moon.)

As you can see, the Cross Spread thoroughly considers all angles of an issue. The first and second cards reveal the heart of the matter. The third and seventh cards show what's going on inside the querent, while the fourth and eighth demonstrate what's surrounding the querent. The fifth and ninth cards tell us about the querent's past, and the six and tenth cards focus on the querent's future and the main message for the querent. The Cross Spread and the Tarot's astrological roots are further explored in *The Alchemy of Tarot: Practical Enlightenment through the Astrology, Qabalah, and Archetypes of Tarot*; also a detailed resource for more advanced astrological and Qabalistic Tarot spreads.

QUESTIONS REQUIRING YES OR NO ANSWERS

It is not the purpose of a Tarot deck to tell the querent what to do in a particular situation, but instead to give him or her more information so that she/he may see more clearly, and thus make better decisions. Generally, it is not a good idea to make any decision when emotionally upset, physically weakened—by hunger, illness, or sleep deprivation—or when one knows that she/he is not seeing clearly. However, let's say that you don't have much time, and you just need a quick *yes* or *no* to a simple question like, "Is this price quoted by the mechanic the best I will find?"

Shuffle and cut the cards the way you always do, and pull one card off the top of the deck.

- If the card is upright and positive, the answer is "yes."
- If the card is reversed and positive, the answer is "yes—but wait before acting."
- If, on the other hand, the card is upright but its meaning is either negative or mixed, the answer is "no."
- If the card is reversed and either negative or mixed, a simple "yes" or "no" is not sufficient to answer the question; thus, a more comprehensive spread is necessary.

QUESTIONS OF TIME

Invariably, a concerned querent will ask the question, "When?" Although often crucial to a complete answer, be very careful and precise before responding to this question—make sure you know; it is always appropriate to admit that you do not. Then again, an experienced reader can use the Tarot to accurately answer questions of time. Only answer questions of time within the context of a reading; allow a preponderance of information to guide you.

There are two basic methods for determining the timing of an event; below I will list and explain them in order of difficulty.

BASIC TIME MEASUREMENT:

1. SEASONS OF THE YEAR:

This method works well for more simple Tarot Spreads. Each Suit in the Tarot relates to a particular season of the year:

Wands are Spring, Cups are Summer, Swords are Autumn, and Pentacles are Winter. Use the Tarot suits to predict timing within the coming year.

For example, if there is a predominance of Wands in a reading (more than half), then the event in question will happen in Spring. The aces of each suit suggests the start of the corresponding season.

Additionally, each season of the year encompasses three signs of zodiac: Aries, Taurus, and Gemini occur in the Spring; Cancer, Leo, and Virgo arise in the Summer; Libra, Scorpio, and Sagittarius happen in Autumn; finally, Capricorn, Aquarius, and Pisces emerge in Winter.

If three or more zodiacal signs of a particular season appear in a reading, this can indicate that the event will occur during the corresponding season (or even more specifically, if two or more cards correlating to one specific Sign appear in a reading, then the event will happen during the corresponding time period attributed to the Sign).

2. TYPES OF SIGNS:

To know how long something will last or how long the querent will have to wait, look for a majority of types of signs of the zodiac in a reading:

Cardinal Signs (Aries, Cancer, Libra, Capricorn)—weeks/ short time span

Fixed Signs (Taurus, Leo, Scorpio, Aquarius)—years/ long time span

Mutable Signs (Gemini, Virgo, Sagittarius, Pisces)—unable to determine/ medium or unknown time span.

Conclusion

The Kingdom Within Tarot is a vital tool created to impart insights into your life's struggles and circumstances, as well as enhance your own inner journey as you explore the Kingdom of Heaven that can only be found within; may it serve you well, yet never replace your own willingness to see clearly and act appropriately. No tool replaces the common sense, intellect, intuition, and talents of the person who wields it; instead, use *The Kingdom Within Tarot* deck to artfully craft yourself into the joyful masterpiece you are meant to be!

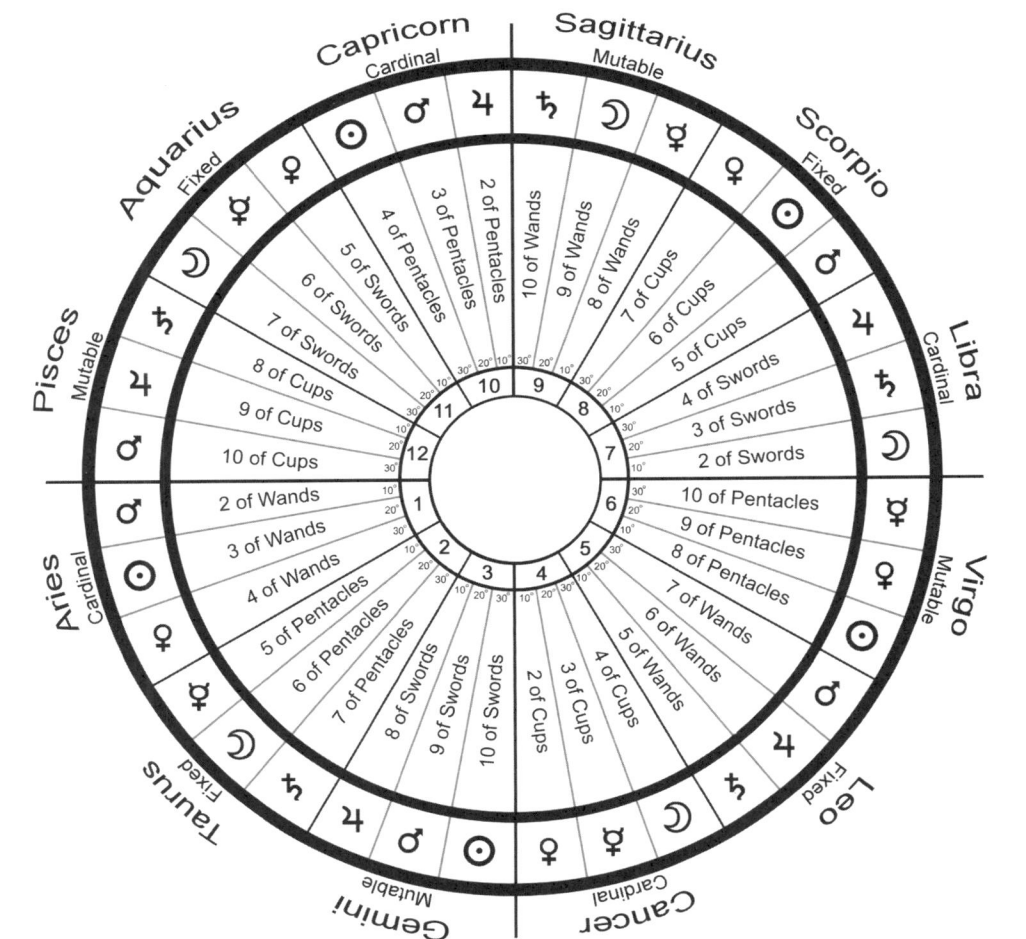

About the Author

Juno Lucina

Ever fluid and changing, Juno is more a verb than a noun, more a blank canvas than an outcome. She wishes that All awaken from Vishnu's dream, to see All That Is. Juno is just a Story pointing the Way.

About the Illustrator

Shannon ThornFeather

Shannon has been a practicing Ceremonial Magician, Ontologist and student of Metaphysics for more than fifteen years. She currently enjoys the wonder and mystery that life is as she works and plays in southern California with her best friend, Jeff.